THE
HALF-TIMBER HOUSE

ITS ORIGIN, DESIGN, MODERN PLAN, AND CONSTRUCTION

ILLUSTRATED WITH PHOTOGRAPHS OF OLD EXAMPLES AND AMERICAN ADAPTATIONS OF THE STYLE

BY

ALLEN W. JACKSON

NEW YORK
McBRIDE, NAST & COMPANY
1912

Published March, 1912

Printing Statement:

Due to the very old age and scarcity of this book,
many of the pages may be hard to read due to the
blurring of the original text, possible missing pages,
missing text, dark backgrounds and other issues
beyond our control.

Because this is such an important and rare work, we
believe it is best to reproduce this book regardless of
its original condition.

Thank you for your understanding.

THE HALF-TIMBER HOUSE

THE COUNTRY HOUSE LIBRARY
A SERIES OF ARCHITECTURAL BOOKS
FOR THE LAYMAN

THE COUNTRY HOUSE LIBRARY

BUNGALOWS   *By Henry H. Saylor*

THE HALF-TIMBER HOUSE
                    By Allen W. Jackson

CONCRETE AND STUCCO HOUSES
                    By Oswald C. Hering

ARCHITECTURAL STYLES FOR COUNTRY
    HOMES
            A symposium by prominent architects

IN PREPARATION

RECLAIMING THE OLD HOUSE
                By Charles Edward Hooper

THE DUTCH COLONIAL HOUSE
                By Aymar Embury, II.

FURNISHING THE HOME OF GOOD TASTE
                By Lucy Abbot Throop

THE COLONIAL HOUSE
                By Joseph Everett Chandler

HOMES THAT ARCHITECTS HAVE BUILT
    FOR THEMSELVES
                By the Architects and Others

McBRIDE, NAST & COMPANY, PUBLISHERS

TO

ALL THOSE

WHO OWN

CASTLES IN SPAIN

Half-timber work of the present day is seen at its best in conjunction with other materials, where the contrasting pattern between the plaster and the wood work is kept very simple, or restricted to use for features of the building that need accent.

Contents

The Illustrations

Preface

THIS book is not intended as a technical treatise. It has not been written with the professional reader in mind and is without pretention to be a serious contribution to the history of architecture. It is addressed primarily to the general reader having an interest in house building or to those who have in mind building for themselves.

If it serves to call the attention of any such to this English work or to arouse their interest in the matter as a whole, it will have fulfilled its purpose. In the mind of the author it is further meant to be at once a protest against the stereotyped use of certain historical styles for contemporary use, and a plea for a greater freshness and virility than is often found in the work of to-day.

It would be impossible to acknowledge all the sources of information drawn upon, but mention should be made of S. O. Aldy's *The Evolution of the English House*, J. A. Gotch's *History of the Early Renaissance in England,* and the various works of P. H. Litchfield. Nor must the author omit to express his thanks to the Publishers of *Country Life* (London), *The Architectural Review* and B. T. Batsford, for the use of illustrations owned by them.

Chapter III. is largely taken from a previous article which appeared in *House and Garden.*

After much hesitation the author has illustrated some of his own work. He has been led to do this not because of its supposed merit, but rather because it happened to illustrate certain points which he wished to make, better than any other work of which illustrations were available.

ALLEN W. JACKSON

202 BRATTLE ST., CAMBRIDGE
November 30, 1911

THE
HALF-TIMBER
HOUSE

Introduction

THE whole question of so-called " style " in architecture is an interesting one for the student. There exists an intelligent opinion that the architectural styles of the past are dead, and that it is a servile and barren archaism to persist in working over old forms; which, because the causes of their being have ceased to operate, have become lifeless material, and the result moribund and an obstruction to real advance in architecture and esthetics. While it is true that the conditions which gave birth to, and differentiated, the architectural styles have lost their force, they have at the same time become so broadened and made free that any of the styles may now be properly used where their characteristics do not render them impracticable from the utilitarian point of view. This is the only excuse for the eclecticism of the present day.

The differences and peculiarities of the various styles were due to climate, to materials at hand, and to the peculiarities of the civilization under which they came into existence. Let us consider briefly a typical Italian farmhouse. The material is stone, both because that was the material easiest to be had and because it would keep out the heat of summer. The windows are small, the cornices overhang widely — to keep out the excessive light of a southern sun. The result, if we go no farther, is a certain type of house, the logical outgrowth of fulfilling the requirements in the easiest way. With an English farm we find the same logical result. In the stone country of the north the buildings are of stone; in the timber country of the south, of timber; and because of the many dull gray days they all, unlike the Italian houses, coax the sun with plenty of windows and little or no cornice with its accompanying shadow. Thus working along the lines pointed out by necessity and convenience, each arrived at a perfect architectural expression of his own condition, requirements, and point of view. This development was still further kept a mirror of the peculiar genius and environment of the builders by their ignorance of what others were doing. The English carpenter never saw the Italian roof or the Spanish *patio,* and was not tempted to experiment in these things. His building was unaffected. His very limitations were a source of strength, and the difference in the result correctly measures the racial differences between one country and another. This is as it should be, and a real style is the inevitable result. In this way only can an architectural style be formed.

Now let us look at the case in this country. Can we have a United States style of architecture? Our architecture will differentiate itself from that of other countries, in just so much as our type and degree of civilization is different from theirs. It will be as individual and peculiar as the demands, and our ability to fulfill them, are peculiar and individual.

In the twentieth century such differences are all very slight among the more highly civilized nations. Not only is there a similarity in requirement and an equal facility in building skill, but the building materials of the world are equally accessible to all. The requirements of the life led by a gentleman in New York, London, Paris, and Vienna nowadays are much the same. All desire to live on the same kind of well policed street. Their business and social lives are much alike. All wear the same sort of clothes, heat their houses in the same way; modern sanitary appliances are common to all; all have electric light; all live secure and peaceful lives. The powerful families of New York do not need a fortified tower into which to gather their households when the hirelings of a rival house come charging around the corner. The gentleman on the Champs Elysées does not need a moat and drawbridge, or contrivances to greet the guest with molten lead. The Viennese citizen no longer builds his house with a watchtower, on the top of a precipitous rock. Any of these gentlemen can build of what material he pleases or can afford

"The Gables," Thelwall, England. In spite of the large amount of timbering a harsh contrast has been avoided by keeping the color of the wood light

It is an extremely easy matter to miss the mark in half-timber work, even when skill and money are available — note the symmetry of the design and the character of the windows, neither of which is in keeping with good half-timber work

— wood, stone, brick, tile or steel are equally within the reach of all. Structurally then their houses will be much alike, and as decoration should be the direct outgrowth of structure, and clothe the skeleton with grace and beauty without denying the existence of the bones, there is no reason for any logical difference in appearances. Such differences as exist are the measure of the distance we have still to travel to reach the perfect cosmopolitanism. The local inherited forms and motives of decoration are nowadays no better known to the builders of any locality than are those of all the rest of the world, since the labors of Mr. Daguerre and Mr. Thomas Cook have made us all so wise. There will be perforce, much interchange and borrowing according to individual preference, and it becomes a question of individual taste in style rather than a rigidly imposed national one.

Another great source of freedom is the gain in structural material. In the old days of brick, stone, mortar, wood and tile, the ambitions of him who would soar were held down by the very limited powers of those materials. A stone will cover but a small opening, and even an arch stretched to the extent of those found in the Roman baths, pays a great price in space and weight for its still limited span. Timber has an even more restricted usefulness in size and strength, as well as in durability. The same is true of columns which hold the superstructure, and even the attenuation attained by the Gothic builders in their most daring work soon reached its limitations. But nowadays, since Mr. Carnegie has put a wand of steel into the hands of the builder, he has become something very like a magician, and if he does not quite build castles in the air, he at least approaches very near it, and is daily growing to have less and less respect for the old-fashioned law of gravitation. Chimneys and towers which formerly had to start from the ground, may now begin in the attic and are not allowed below stairs where they get in the way. Great auditoriums may be placed in the centre of buildings, with a dozen floors of offices over the ceiling. Supports are in disgrace and are either done away with or relegated to out-of-the-way corners. And as for height, who shall say?

With all the world, then, having equal access to all the materials of building, with housing requirements varying but little, with each builder perfectly familiar with the architectural monuments and history of the world, there seems but a sorry chance of any United States style. It would require a new, radical, unheard-of departure in our mode of living to bring forward demands so novel that they could be met only by fresh discoveries in materials or methods to really constitute a new style.

It would seem, then, that if we are to have new styles of architecture, they will be world-wide and mark new advances in building material, or new and extraordinary housing problems.

Meanwhile there is plenty of room for individual genius to exercise itself with the creation of beauty in building, and to this there is no end, for if there are nine and sixty methods of constructing tribal lays, there are certainly as many of conceiving each of nine and sixty different sorts of buildings. If we are sometimes tempted to complain that we are born too late and that all the changes have been rung on four walls and a roof, we may find some comfort in Sir Joshua Reynolds' remark that " Art comes by a kind of felicity and not by rule," in which case we need not fear of exhausting its possibilities.

A carefully designed house at Bryn Mawr, Pa., that is satisfying even without the help that
may be expected later from its surroundings

Duhring, Okie & Ziegler, Architects

An old farmhouse at Chaumont

A royal playhouse, Versailles. While the French half-timber work is interesting,
it does not belong to us in the way that the half-timber houses of England do

History of English Domestic Architecture

WHILE what are known as " Half-timber " buildings are equally indigenous to England, France and Germany, it is with the work in England that we shall chiefly concern ourselves. While the French and German work is of just as high a type and of equal interest to the student of architecture, for us it is a " foreign " style in a sense in which the more ethnic work of England is not. In the half-timber houses of England were born, lived and died our own great-grandfathers; these houses were conceived and wrought out by our own progenitors; they are our architectural heritage, our homesteads, and hold an important place in our building history.

This is not true of the German and French work, which is strange and foreign to us in its motives and feeling, with nothing in common with the Island work but the name. It has had no influence on our own work, and is entirely outside the story of the English and American home with which we purpose to concern ourselves in this book. This timber work of the Continent is in fact an excellent example of how the same materials used for the same end, in the hands of men of different genius, produce a result that in each case takes its color from the mind of its creator — it is a subtle document, a bit of racial evidence of the atmosphere that surrounds it.

Half-timber work, or, as it is often called, " black-and-white," is sometimes defined by English writers as that sort of building in which the first story is of masonry and of which the second story only is timbered; when the whole building is timbered it is properly called " all-timbered." This is not the commonly accepted idea of most architects, who understand by the term " half-timber " that the whole or part of the building is constructed with a timber frame filled in with brick, mortar, or something of the sort, that produces the effect of " black " stripes on a white wall. This is " black-and-white " work, or, if looked at from the builder's point of view, half timber and half filling.

This method of building is very old. It is easy to see how it came into being as an outgrowth of the more primitive work which preceded it, and was the natural outcome of following the lines of least resistance, with no thought of what it would look like or where it would lead. It is evident that it did not become the vogue because stripes happened to be the fashion, but for the much more satisfactory reason that it was the simplest, easiest, and quickest way of getting a house, and fulfilled the few necessary requirements.

Although there are probably not standing to-day any half-timber houses older than the fifteenth century, there is no doubt that houses of this character were being built for a hundred years before that time. The oldest half-timber houses we have left to-day are often disguised in a strange dress and are made to pass themselves off as having tile walls, or are boarded in with wide horizontal deal boards. The reason for this is not a desire to deceive, but because " it prolongs the life, and is just as good," as benzoate of soda is used with old fruit. In cases of this sort it is ugliness that is only skin deep, and our honest great timbers, silvered with age, are just beneath the surface. The frames were ordinarily of oak, which as it first shrunk and then decayed, not only pulled away from the mortar filling but opened up mortises and presented gaping joints to the weather, racking the building and making it in course of time uninhabitable. To make the walls tight without rebuilding, the expedient was adopted of strapping them and hanging on tile, or boarding the surface, and in this way continuing the life and usefulness of the structure.

This type of work is not found all over England, but only in the timbered districts, or what formerly were the timbered districts — roughly speaking, in the central, western, and southern portions. In the north, stone has always been the first thing at hand and was universally used for both walls and roofing, even in the small cottages. In the south, with timber went excellent clay for making tile and brick, and these were both much used, although at a later date, as we find no mention of brick before 1400, and tile was probably coeval with it.

Before considering the half-timber work proper, let us see what preceded it and of what it was the outgrowth and legitimate successor. The earliest houses of which we have any real knowledge, were formed by the placing of great crucks, which were the naturally curved trunks of trees, with their bases some distance

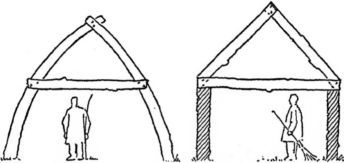

Fig. 1. The frames of the earliest houses, formed with the curved trunks of trees

Fig. 2. The next step was to put a wall under this roof, gaining an attic

apart, and sloping them toward each other until the tops met. The tops were fastened together and the pair braced by what we should now call a collar beam, the whole forming a letter A (see Fig. 1). A similar frame was set up at a convenient distance, and the two joined with purlins, the outside of these sloping walls or roof — for they were both one and the other — being further braced and joined with smaller structural filling, and then entirely covered and made tight against the weather by thatch, slates or whatever came to hand. Sometimes transepts called " shots " were constructed at right angles to gain more space. An ordinary building consisted of several of these bays. The determination of the proper spacing of these pairs of crucks forming bays is interesting, and typical of the kind of pressing utilitarian requirements which dictate the direction and mold the growth of architectural style. It has been observed of them that they were always spaced about sixteen feet apart. This distance is exactly that required for the stabling of a double yoke of oxen, which was the team commonly used in plowing at the time these houses were built. The projection of the cruck into the room would naturally indicate the place for a division or partition. As a further bit of evidence that these bays were a proper width for the stabling of cattle we find that the Latin writers on agriculture lay it down as a rule that a pair of oxen should occupy what is the equivalent of eight feet, and it is interesting to see that in a far distant country, and after an interval of a thousand years, the thickness of an ox has not changed; so that if he is evolving at all it must be in the direction of his length. The houses of this period are always spoken of in the old deeds in terms of bays, that is, as being six bays, or four and one-half bays and so on.

It might also be noted in passing that our field measure, the rod, is derived in the same way, and is the space taken up by four oxen plowing abreast. To make our farms produce not only all material things necessary to life, but an abstract system of mensuration as well, is keeping our feet on the ground pretty consistently. There is something typically Anglo-Saxon about deriving our system of measures from the size of oxen and the tillage of the soil, just as the logical and scientific mind of the Gaul is seen in his taking the mathematically determined circumference of the earth as his unit of measurement.

This matter of the spacing of the crucks to form bays in these early stables is of interest because the architectural influence of the ox persists long after the time when the Englishman's house was not only his castle but his stable as well. Even when this primitive arrangement was outgrown and the man separated from his beast, the old sixteen-foot spacing of the bays continued in the great halls of the nobility and gentry, even into the large and luxurious manors which sprang up all over the land during the sixteenth century, and as late as the end of the Tudor Period

A cottage at Hetherington, Leicestershire, which is particularly interesting as a
survival of the earliest form of timber construction

"Compton Wynyates," a typical manor house hall with the minstrels' gallery

— the heyday of the building arts in England. At a time when your carpenter would have scratched his head in vain if asked why he spaced his bays this particular width, it had passed into a building tradition and become one of the rule-of-thumb methods of laying out a building. This curious detail only disappears when the unaffected indigenous Anglo-Saxon method of building was itself crushed out of existence forever by the superimposition of the alien style from Italy which had been making its influence felt from its first appearance in the time of Henry VIII. down to its complete ascendancy at the hands of Inigo Jones in the early part of the seventeenth century. Up to the time of the appearance of this exotic fashion the cause of native art had marched on in an uninterrupted course, having a natural, logical development, keeping pace with the advancing civilization and solving its new problems as they arose, in the light of the accumulated experience inherited from past ages.

But to return to our building, half house, half barn and stable, with its sixteen-foot bays. In the larger ones the cattle stood down either side for more than half the length, facing out, as one sees them to-day in our New England barns. In the middle near the end, and blocking up the aisle, was the fireplace, and behind that the master's rooms, the " bower " and often another room or two. For a long time the " fireplace " was that and nothing more, merely a spot in the centre of the aisle where the fire which served for heat and where all the cooking was done, blazed away on a few flat stones innocent of any such effete contrivance as back, sides or flue. To be sure, a hole in the roof was made as a concession to the smoke, but it was expected to find it unassisted, which, unless smoke has changed its habits, one may believe it did in a somewhat leisurely and roundabout fashion. Chimneys, in the sense we now understand the word, were hardly known in England until the fourteenth century. Even the larger halls and manors had their fires in the centre of the room and allowed the smoke to find its way out through an opening in the roof, which was when necessary guarded against the entrance of the weather by louvres.   Later the fires were built against the stone walls of the room and covered by a great projecting hood, sometimes of stone, sometimes of metal, and often of " daub " or mud plaster on wickerwork.   This collected the smoke which was carried off by a flue set against the wall and running up through the roof.   This flue was built of the same materials, and undoubtedly one of the reasons why so few traces of flues in the old buildings are found is because of their construction of such inflammable material.   Laws were finally passed forbidding flues to be built having any wood about them.

Up to this point the building is all roof, or at least wall and roof are one, whichever we choose to call it, but as skill in building increased and the demands were for something more elaborate, it was easy to put a wall under this roof and raise it into the air and thus gain an attic (Fig. 2), also to add a shed roof on either side parallel to the centre aisle like the transepts of a basilican church, and so gain in width as well.

The servants slept in lofts over the cattle, the men on one side, the maids on the other.   In such an intimate gathering of man and beast under one roof the all-pervading wood smoke must have been a real blessing, serving as it undoubtedly did in a great measure as a deodorizer and insecticide.

Even after the cattle had been given a building to themselves and the lords of the manor had begun to live with some pomp and circumstance in their own houses, the servants of both sexes slept on the floor of the great hall of the manor, which was the dining-room and general meeting-place during the day.   This promiscuity was the cause of much ribald wit in the song and story of the Middle Ages.

While for the purpose of planning our buildings to-day it is perhaps of little practical assistance to trace the history of English house planning, it is of some interest to the student of domestic architecture to follow the development of the plan and note how each step is in answer to some developed need, and to fulfil

and meet some condition that has arisen. As this logical and inevitable growth and change are the blood and bones of our architectural style, or rather *are* the style, we shall not arrive at a clear
and correct understanding of half-timber work as we see it
to-day in England unless we do look somewhat into the conditions
under which it was produced. While this will be done more
fully elsewhere, it should not be uninteresting or uninstructive
to follow the development of the plan a little further than the
half barn, half house of the yeoman and franklin, and see how
their betters fared.

In the turbulent times of the Middle Ages it was necessary
that every man's house should be a fortress as well. We see even
to-day the crags and hilltops of Europe capped with castles or
ruins of former strongholds which relied largely on their inacces-
sibility for immunity from attack. They were usually built surrounding a courtyard, so that in time of siege the defenders might
have some place to take the air. When, however, we leave the
mountainous countries and come to France and England — flat
lands with no strategic height on which to perch a fortress-
dwelling, we find men surrounding their houses with water in
lieu of precipitous and rocky cliffs, as a means of keeping off the
marauder. The fosse, or moat, as we know it in England, made
the insular Britain still more insular, and gave him an excellent
substitute for the lofty perch of his Continental brother. Like
him, however, and for the same reason, he keeps the courtyard in
the centre.

As time goes on, and a more peaceable era succeeds the earlier
riotous conditions, the first movement toward the disarmament
of the house is the knocking out of the front side of the rectangular building so that the court is exposed, and the U-shaped
building appears. From the usual fact of a small porch in the
centre of the cross wing, forming a slight projection in plan, it
is more often spoken of as the E type of plan. The pretty theory
that this was an architectural compliment to Queen Elizabeth,
in whose reign many houses of this sort first appeared, will not

stand the test of historic research, and a stage in matter-of-fact evolution can hardly be turned to such sycophantic account.

The corners of the typical old rectangle often were marked by towers which remained to accent the ends of the U when the front side of the rectangle was removed. Now the sides of the U, or wings of the house, disappear, or at least give place to a mere fence or wall, and the towers remain standing at some distance from the house, while in the effete times of long-continued peace they became merely garden or tool houses. To complete the dwindling of the old pile, the towers finally follow the rest, and we have nothing but a slender fence to mark where the embattled walls once stood. Thus we shear our castle till there is left but a simple home with an enfenced yard in front; and it is this memory of medieval usage that our forefathers brought to this country in the fenced and gate-posted front yards of the Colonial dwellings which we see still standing, up and down the Atlantic seaboard.

This then, in brief, is the typical course taken by the cottage on the one hand and the castle on the other, down through the Middle Ages in England, as they were acted upon by Time with his train of attendant circumstance, all the products of a changing condition of men and things. Responding truly to the logic of events it continued, by the force of such adaptation, to keep alive and to be a growing, living organism, until fashion roughly superceded it with an imported alien style.

The gateway of St. John's Hospital, Canterbury — showing the sturdy architecture
that was produced without striving after picturesqueness

A gate house, Stokesay, Shropshire — a fine example of the best work where the enrichment has been judiciously introduced

The Half-timber House in England

NOW let us suppose that a small but prosperous farmer of the year 1500 wishes to build a comfortable house for himself and his family somewhere in the south of England. He will scorn the idea of admitting cattle under the same roof, as his forefathers did, and is able to afford a house of some comfort, even luxury. He will have a large room for living and eating, with great fireplace and ingle, window-seat and row of glazed and leaded windows, a low, heavily beamed ceiling and a floor of tile or flags.

In the old work the fireplaces, after they had retreated from the middle of the floor in the fourteenth century and backed up against the wall, adopted the luxury of a flue to collect and guide the smoke in a straight and narrow way out of the room and house. They were big honest affairs, bespeaking plenty of dry split logs in the shed; glorious great smoked caverns, which were kitchen range, hot-water boiler and heating system all in one and the centre and heart of the house as they deserved to be. There is nothing more pleasant, wholesome and hearty than the way in which in song and story, art and history, the English " hearth " and " home " are linked together. The chimney corner was the lounging-room, library, study, and smoking-room, and the history of English house-planning swings about this as a pivot. It is the anchor of the whole.

The farmer will have an entry-way and stairs near the centre; buttery, kitchen and pantries to one side. On the second floor, under the roof, he will have bedrooms with their windows close under the eaves, or higher, so that the eaves must sweep up over them. The hall or corridor from which bedrooms may lead was an idea that waited long before it came crashing into the mind of some thoughtful planner — one of those simple expedients that it takes a great man to discover and for the lack of which all sorts of inconveniences in social intercourse were endured, and human progress in social adjustment itself held back. The inventor of the corridor deserves a statue as much as does Eli Whitney or James Watt, instead of filling an unknown grave. It was not only the humble farmer who must pass through some one else's room to get out of his own in those days, but lords in their castles

The chimney-corner was from the first the centre and heart of the English Home

and kings in their palaces put up with having their suites of rooms turned into passageways. It is the same in France, Germany and Italy. We find sumptuous suites of rooms in great houses, but all strung together in a way that the modern flat-hunting young couple would pronounce " impossible." That it was felt to be a great inconvenience is shown by the clumsy expedient, in many of the old houses, of having a number of staircases both inside and out to serve as a sort of dignified ladder by which one might leave his bedroom without embarrassing his neighbors.

However, our canny farmer at least puts this inconvenience to some practical use, for he and his gudewife take for themselves the room at the head of the stairs, with maids on one side and the men on the other, so that he commands the junction, and can keep strict watch of the comings and goings.

His first floor will be perhaps of earth, not even stopping to remove the top loam, and this will pack down and make a surface not too smooth, to be sure, and certainly none too clean. If the ground should prove to be damp he will have a foul place to live in, at least according to modern notions. It is certainly a long way from waxed oak, and a vacuum cleaner. If he wishes something more pretentious he will have for flooring uncut stone laid without mortar and fitted together as closely as possible.

For the second floor he must needs use boards to span the joists, and he will use wide oak ones; planks they might more properly be called, from their thickness. First thick reeds will be laid across the joists, then the boards on top nailed down through the reeds. Now he can plaster the ceiling between the joists, the reeds forming the lath, and he will have not only a tight floor but one with some pretense to being sound-proof. In some districts it has been found that they have gone one step further and left off the board flooring, and, instead, covered the reeds as they lay across the joists, above and below, thoroughly embedding them in a four-inch or five-inch sheet of plaster that attains the hardness of cement. We thus see our ferro-concrete methods anticipated by half a millenary, for if the reeds were iron rods we should have the very latest American invention in reinforced fireproof flooring.

The roof he will probably cover with thatch a foot or two in thickness, made of rye straw, and if he is afraid of fire he may give it a coat of whitewash, the lime affording considerable protection against the flames. Fire is the great enemy of thatch, for in a prolonged drought the straw becomes like tinder and shrinks away from the dirt, moss, etc., which perforce are present, forming a sort of tinder, and rendering it an even more easy prey to

fire. At an early period in London it was one of the building laws
that all thatch must be kept whitewashed, and it became so common throughout England that the villages with their white roofs
sparkling in the sun must have presented a very different picture
from what we see to-day in the hamlets where thatch is still to be
found.

Let us suppose, however, that the farmer does not wish to use
thatch for the roof. He may use tile made by hand, of an excellent quality and burnt to a pleasant red of varying shades. In
the districts where the proper clays were to be found, tile was a
very popular method of covering not only roofs but walls. Often
when the oak beams of a half-timber house had so shrunk or rotted
from the effects of age and weather that the filling had disinte-
grated and the whole structure was no longer proof against wind
and weather, instead of repairing along the same lines, which
would be a difficult thing to do, they hung the walls with tile, and
many a Kent and Surrey tile-covered farmhouse of to-day is
really an old half-timber building in a new dress. These tile
were, of course, hand-made, and as a consequence possessed a certain unevenness of texture, which when added to the fact that the
hanging holes were far from being punched with mathematical
exactness, gave the wall on which they were hung a softness of
surface which was most pleasing, accidental and fortuitous though
it was. These tile were thicker than those we get to-day, and, as
was to be expected along with the other imperfect methods of
manufacture, came in a great variety of color, produced by the
uneven burning in the kiln. The tile were often cut with a
rounded or curved butt, so that the builders were fond of getting
variety by laying first several rows of the curved, and then several
rows of straight ends. These tile, like the slate, were hung with
wooden pins which of course in time rotted and gave way,
but could be easily replaced, and in a country where there was
no severe frost or heavy snowfall, they were perfectly suited to
their purpose.

If, however, the builder has an objection to tile, he may, if he

An admirable example of the charm of soft texture that resulted in the old work
from the fact that it was not built with mathematical exactness

The sticks are vertical in the earlier work and rather close together, there
being about as much plaster showing as wood

happens to live in the right district, cover his roofs with slate or other flat stone, roughly split, heavy but durable, defying fire and frost, and presenting a fine, substantial appearance. To be sure he must make the rafters strong and tie them well, for this roof will never sleep, but its constant pressure will need stout work below to keep it in the air. However, there will be no lack of heavy timber of solid oak. Two-by-four-inch spruce studs are an invention of a more architecturally anaemic age. The pitch of the roof was determined empirically by striking a medium between a flatness that threw the great weight of the stone full on the rafters and called for great strength in them, and the steeper roof that caused the stones to drag heavily on their wooden pins and in time pull loose and fall to the ground. As a result of these conflicting problems we usually find as a matter of fact that the roofs which are, or were meant to be, covered with stone are flatter than the tile or thatch roofs.

The stone was laid over a layer of straw. The ridge was formed either with a saddle board of rolled lead, or often with a continuous row of overlapping half-roll tiles embedded in mortar. The use of flashing (thin sheet metal used to make tight the edges and joints with chimneys, end walls, etc.) is really a confession of weakness, and the old builders got along with surprisingly little of it.

Now we have our roof and floors; let us consider what kind of wall he will have to hold them up. There is little building stone at hand, and he certainly will not propose to bring material of one sort from a distance when he has another perfectly good sort at hand. Brick is not yet in common use and not well understood, but what he does have in abundance is timber. The hills are covered with fine oak trees, than which no finer building wood has ever existed. Here it is, ready to hand, and here are the axes and broad-axes and men who have the proper handling of them as an inheritance from untold generations. If they are not born with an ax in their hands, one finds itself there very shortly. So then he will begin to chop; now it does not take many hours with an ax, squaring up the trunk of a tree, to learn that it is easier to make one's timbers large than small. It is as much, if not more, bother to get out a thin plank, than it is a great stick; and so he will save time and use the big timbers. With their great size and strength he may well space them some distance apart, and fill in between with something or other not so hard to make as planks. For this purpose he will use a mortar or " daub " made of lime and straw, or clay and twigs, or anything that will stick and harden, and reasonably resist the weather, which is not rigorous or one that makes great demands on building materials. As a groundwork for lathing for this plaster he will weave willow twigs together and make a groove in the sides of his timber to take

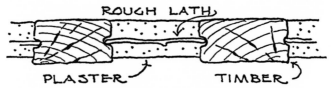

Woven willow twigs, engaging in grooves in the timber, form a support for the plaster

the ends and make a tighter bond between the filling and the beams, so that if the timber does shrink away there will not be an open crack straight through the wall. Then if he plasters the inside of the wall all over he will be as snug as possible. He may make it a more substantial wall by using as a filling brickbats, small stones or what-not, and covering the whole with plaster.

In place of the plaster filling we sometimes find brick laid up in a herringbone pattern, set in mortar and left to show their red surfaces framed between the gray timbers.

For the corner posts a baulk was used, cut near the foot of the tree to get the beginning of the sweeping curve where it runs out into the roots. These sticks were turned upside down and the curved end formed the bracket to support the girt for the over-hanging second story, while the crooked branches were used for the curved struts and braces. An old writer, Harrison, says, " No oke can grow so crooked but it falleth out to some use." It

An interesting example showing the use of brick filling between the timbers,
laid horizontally.   Where brick was employed it was usually
laid in a diagonal pattern

An old house in Rouen in which the brick filling between the timbers is laid in an interesting pattern

Notice the overhang of the stories. It is not quite clear why this was almost universally done

is not quite clear why this almost universal overhang was adopted for the upper stories, at least in the country districts. In the cities these successive overhangs as the stories were added one above another formed an excellent shelter from the rain for the

Brick was frequently used as the material for filling in between the timbers, laid up in a variety of patterns

shop front on the street, and it was not uncommon for houses on the opposite sides of city streets to bow gravely to each other in this way until they approached so near that those in the attic windows could shake hands across the street.

There is no doubt that these offsets gained for the framework a certain amount of stiffness, and it may have been for this reason that they were adopted; whatever the reason, the introduction into the design of this horizontal band of shadow and the very marked division of the stories which it represents, added a most pleasing feature to the whole whether or not introduced with that idea. Our pleasure is largely due, no doubt, to its engaging candor in letting us into the secrets of its interior arrangement to that extent.

This then is the original method of making these walls, perfectly logical, following the lines of least resistance, and utilizing what comes to hand. It is like all good architecture in that it is the by-product of honest building.

Thus we have the result of our farmer's work in " black-and-white " walls of " half-timber." The sticks are vertical in the earlier work and close together, there being about as much plaster showing as wood. In the later work, where the timbers are placed further apart, we have more " white " and less " black," and then, as they became more facile, the builders amused themselves with arranging the upright timbers and sticks to form diverse and ingenious patterns, so that we get the quatrefoil, cusps, diamonds with concave sides, and an almost infinite variety of arrangement, in addition to the more sober placing of the sticks. These timbers are all dowelled, the uprights into the sills and the horizontal pieces into the uprights, and pinned with oak pins, the ends of which are left projecting a half-inch or so, that they may be still further driven in should the joints loosen and need to be drawn tighter together. In fact the poorer class of work, the jerry-building of the time, is described as " without augur holes." In some of the work the plaster is kept flush with the face of the timber outside, but as this makes the slightest crack between the two much in evidence, a sinking of the plaster a quarter of an inch or so back of the face not only made this less prominent but gave the whole surface more variety and a more solid and rugged appearance. The feeling of texture in this old work is of course enormously enhanced by the rough surfaces of the timber as it comes from the ax, for smooth as they must have seemed to the ax man, they were nothing as compared to the product of the buzz

The timbers were all dowelled together and held by oak pins, the ends of which
are here seen projecting

The builders soon broke away from the use of vertical timbers alone, introducing diverse and ingenious patterns such as the quatrefoil which is seen here

saw. This, with the varying widths of these timber faces and a certain amount of crookedness in the sticks themselves, together with the apparent unconcern of those having the spacing in charge, gives the whole wall a very soft and gracious presence. For us as we see it to-day this is all accentuated by the heavy hand of age and accompanying decay, which have still further softened the lines and blunted the angles, while Nature has crept up around the base, leaving her mark in every cranny. She has laid on her colors with the wind and rain, until the whole with its timber and thatch seems almost to have reverted to the vegetable kingdom and become some new species of giant plant.

The idea that these people were actuated in their work only by the desire to build tight, warm and cheap shelters, with little regard for beauty, cannot be entertained for a moment when we see the amount of carving on molding, barge-boards and wherever there was a chance for enrichment; clearly indicating their love of beauty, their pride in their work, and their willingness to take the time and expense to gratify it.

The details of doors, with their nailheads and strap hinges, the windows with their patterned bars of lead, the giant chimneys bursting into flower at the top, the generous fireplaces, cunningly jointed paneling, and the accompanying details which these builders wrought, guided and directed in the struggle for beauty by an imagination which took its color from the vigorous, vital, struggling age in which it found itself, are worthy of more than a passing glance.

We will now consider whether this is not a style of architecture that is most facile and flexible, and that lends itself most gracefully to the accommodation of our present-day needs.

Is the Half-timber Style Suited to our Needs To-day?

I FEAR that most members of the architectural profession will dissent with some heat from the observation of the mild Thoreau that " There is some of the same fitness in a man's building his own house that there is in a bird's building its own nest." This sounds well enough until we think of some of the stock-jobbers whom we know, having such potentially dangerous things as hammer and nails thrust into their hands and being sent forth to build their nests. True, as Thoreau continues, " Who knows but if men constructed their own dwellings with their own hands, and provided food for themselves honestly enough, the poetic faculty would be universally developed, as birds universally sing when they are so engaged." It is a pretty picture, surely, of these worthy citizens balancing up the dizzy ladder with hods on their shoulders and madrigals on their lips, but I fear that even the "universal development of the poetic faculty" is too high a price for us to pay. While every bird is born an architect, no man is.

If, then, it is a difficult, slow and painful task to learn to build properly, if it requires countless experiments with their attendant failures to learn to use rightly, wisely and economically the material at hand with the tools at hand, the final result thus arrived at must give it almost the force and dignity of a law of nature. When we have followed the thread of common sense in and out and up and down wherever it has led us, without faltering or evasion, we may expect to come out at last into the light and find ourselves in the presence of Architecture.

For it must be understood that this reflection of the prevailing civilization, this mirror of the customs, manners, limitations and

"Stonecroft," a modern English house in which the traditions of timbering and
bold chimney treatment are well observed

There is an indefinable appeal in the English village — an appeal that is particularly strong for those of us whose forefathers have put their own dreams and idealism into their architecture

environment of a race, showing the slow, painful process of the growth and development of a people, is what goes to the making of, and has as a result, what we call a "style" of architecture. And even when it becomes no longer possible truthfully to reflect the customs, requirements, and desires of a people in the old inherited forms — even then we may not talk of a new style, but rather of modifications and adjustments of the present one, the whole problem being one of growth, both in wants and in their fulfillment.

It is as impossible for a people to repudiate its architecture as it would be to deny its literature. A people's architecture fits them and no one else can wear it. We may see much to admire in others but only our own is flesh of our flesh. The particular style that *we* have been born into, developed by our fathers through the centuries, keeping pace with the slow, painful progress of the race, and always a true index of its contemporary condition; a perfect, inarticulate measure of its culture and refinement; this style, this growing embodiment in stone of a people's dreams and idealism, this for us is the Gothic style of England.

The Georgian style, which was brought to this country and flourished here with some modifications under the name of "Colonial" or, as the redundant phrase has it, "Old Colonial," had nothing Georgian about it unless it be that both the architecture and the dynasty were foreign, for it was not an indigenous style of building like the other. It was an imported fashion, an alien style, as little at home in catering to British institutions as we might expect such a typically Latin product to be. It was nothing but the classic architecture of old Rome revived in North Italy in the fifteenth century and brought into England by the devious way of France and Holland, and showing the influence of the countries through which it had passed on its journey. And even if we admit that long custom has served to imbue these borrowed forms with something of the Anglo-Saxon temperament, we have still the inherent unsuitableness of what is an essentially monumental style of architecture set to serve intimate and domestic uses. Its simplicity and dignity are all very well, but they are bound to a tyrannical symmetry, rigid, cold and immutable. We all know the work as it was brought over and done in the Colonies — charming, but a little frigid, dignified but hardly intimate, chaste but often timid, too often described as simple by its admirers when stupid would be the better word: its vocabulary small if select, its canons fixed and rigid, so that its range of effects is of necessity very limited.

We all know the Colonial house — the front door in the centre flanked on either side by the paired windows above and below, each window the exact size of every other. It may be there is a guest room in one corner and a bathroom in the other, but such is not apparent on the surface. We might have liked to have, for comfort and convenience, three windows on one side, and one on the other, some higher or some smaller, but it would be heresy to take such liberties with this austere front. Like the unlucky traveler in the bed of Procrustes, the poor plan is made to fit the elevations by brute force, either by stretching or lopping off.

Now, setting the matter of style aside for the moment, it is an architectural maxim as applicable to a dog kennel as to a palace, since men first piled one stone on another, that the elevations of a building shall express, as best may be, the plan — shall give some inkling not only of what are in a general way the uses of the building, but, further than this, shall indicate the uses of the various parts of that building as seen from without. Let us suppose, for example, that we find ourselves in the square of a strange village; it is not enough that we can tell which building is the public library, which the fire-engine house and which the town hall, for the architecture is not vital or organic unless we can also tell, as we look at them, where the reading-room of the library is, where in the engine house the firemen sleep and where the hose is hung, and in the town hall where the assembly room is located. Of course this cannot be carried into too much detail.

Baker & Dallett, Architects

A modern house in the suburbs of Philadelphia that is well done without obvious effort

J. Russell Pope, Architect

A detail from a gate lodge on Long Island where the true spirit of
English craftsmanship has been revived

A modern American adaptation of the English tradition, illustrating the way in which the exterior may be made to express something of the floor plan

It would be obviously absurd to press this point too far. In general and in a large way, however, it is a valuable architectural truth.

Now returning to our house with the symmetrical Colonial front: how is it possible for the meanest and the most honored rooms to be equally expressed on the exterior by the same thing — the window, for instance? If a given window is a truthful expression of one room, how can it be of the other? We obviously cannot expect such versatility from our openings. When working in the derivatives of the classic style as applied in domestic work, not to be able to tell from the exterior of a house the bathroom from the parlor, the butler's pantry from the ballroom, is a basic defect of style that forces many undesirable compromises that would be unnecessary in a less rigid system. It is not so much that the style is inarticulate as that it knows so few sentences with which to try and express so many ideas. There should not be this conflict between the plan and its elevations by which one must give way to the other, serious sacrifices having to be made before the two can be coaxed into joining hands. In this feud between Truth and Harmony, Utility stands but a sorry chance. The elevations must follow and grow from the plan; they shall express what they shield; they are the effect and not the cause. Beauty must wait on Use, and is only noble when it serves.

If, then, our exteriors will not subordinate themselves, if they are not perfectly tractable and flexible, it is a weakness, and it is this weakness in architectonics that we think exists to a marked extent in the classic style, and one which never appears so disastrously as in the manifold exigencies of modern house-building. If the *entente cordiale* is lacking in the Georgian work between the plan and its elevations, it is, on the other hand, in this very matter that the strength of the true English work of the Tudor period lies, for the rambling timbered or plastered houses of this time, by wholly ignoring symmetry, gain at the very outset an immense freedom. But because symmetry is neglected, we must not for a moment assume that the work is haphazard and allowed to follow its own devices without thought or care for the result. Balance and accent, variety and composition, are consciously or unconsciously seen, or rather felt, everywhere in these buildings.

The plan here may fulfil the most extraordinary requirements, may house the most incongruous matters under one roof. China-closets may come next to chapels, pantries under boudoirs, yet each have every requirement of light, space and convenience fulfilled, with its proper and fitting exterior expression. The ground may be level, sloping or broken, without embarrassing us in the least. There is ·here the best possible understanding between the plan and the elevation — the understanding that the plan is master and that the other must honor and obey.

The result in England, the home of this work and where it is seen at its best, is those soft, beautiful houses which affect us by their perfect repose and harmony, their feeling of rest and simplicity — no stress or striving here, only peace and quiet. Nowhere are there such *homes* as these. There are others surrounded by grander scenery and more complicated landscape — the restless blue of the Mediterranean may murmur at their feet, snowclad mountains and frowning precipices may stand guard over châlets and farms; there is a charm by the sinuous Danube banked with vineyard and studded with mysterious castles whose storied past swathes them in romance; but when the tired traveler, sated with the aggressive beauty of other lands, feels once more the soft air and views the lush vegetation of the English shires with their peaceful, homely villages, he will be ready for their message of peace and quiet. To know them they must be wooed in various moods — when the hawthorn buds powder the hedges and the blossoms are dancing on the trees and the happy streams croon and gurgle to themselves under the· ancient bridges; or, in some quiet pool, throw back the image of the guardian church; when the sinking sun lends a coat of gold to the homely thatch, or when the great smoking chimneys of the cot-

Harvard House, Stratford-on-Avon—an unusually fine example of the town house front, suggesting the loving care that was expended upon the carving

" These houses take their place in the landscape more like some work of Nature than of man, more as if they had grown than as if they were made"

tages are seen through the gaunt, winter limbs — " Bare ruin'd choirs, where late the sweet birds sang."

These houses take their place in the landscape more like some work of Nature than of man, more as if they had grown than as if they were made, nestling among the trees and verdure like the flower of some larger plant. Rules of the books, precepts of the schools, seem very artificial, thin and profitless in their presence. These buildings have no acquaintance with the paint shop or the planing-mill; they are offsprings of the soil, with their brick and mortar from the fields, and rough-hewn timbers dragged from the forest. As a tree lacks symmetry but possesses perfect balance, so do they. They are not designed under an artificial rule derived from nothing in nature. Neither does their enrichment of detail consist of motives copied from those on Greek temples invented for use five hundred years before Christ. What detail and ornament they have chosen to beautify and deck themselves in is their own, wrought out lovingly, invented painfully and slowly with many slips and many failures by the people themselves — always improving and bettering as they come up out of their darkness of ignorance and poverty. Eloquent of a people's history, such houses as these are *owned* by those who live in them, in a very real sense.

The Charm of Old Work and How We may Obtain It

LAYING aside the esthetic point of view, let us consider if these buildings must remain merely interesting specimens of the handicraft of a byegone age, or if it is possible for us to use this style of work to serve our twentieth century needs.

What are we to say to the Plain Business Man with his strong instinctive suspicion of " Art "? He who says he wants no nonsense about his house, no millinery for him; what *he* wants is something to keep out the rain and keep in the heat, plenty of hot water and a light cellar.

Here is the real architectural critic at last! — here the great, patient, primal voice of the World asking for shelter. This is the prophet of the marketplace striving to express the dim, atavic stirrings of his innermost being. Thus Noah spoke to his shipwright; so demanded Paraoh on the fields of Karnak; and Nero thus admonished the builders of the Golden House. And when Ibn-i-Ahmar stood on the Alhambra hill and pointed with his scimitar at the growing Generalife it was in words like these he spoke.

With our half-timber work we need not flinch beneath his gaze, for it can fulfil all his requirements. Nothing can be more practical. We can tell him, first, that his work is perfectly suited to our climate. The plaster makes a warmer house in winter and a cooler in summer than can be had with any of the forms of wood alone; it costs less than brick or stone and, when properly done, even over wooden studs, is very durable. There is no cost of up-keep, and the amount of painting or oiling is restricted to the trim and is negligible. The color and texture of the plaster may be varied considerably and, even when new, is thoroughly

One of the essentials of success in half-timber work is the grouping of windows
rather than leaving them as isolated units

A typical example of the smaller English manors.　Notice here the grouping
of the windows

It is hard to separate the architecture from its setting and from the softening
influences of time, and estimate how much of a composition like this
is really a result of forethought

charming and wonderfully harmonious among the surrounding vegetation.

As for appearance, one must not expect to find in the modern work the charm and fascination which so delight us in the old English crofts and manors, for their charm is largely due to age and nature. It is an exceedingly difficult thing to judge architecture of a byegone time *per se* — that is, to separate the architecture, the conscious design, entirely from its setting, and pass judgment on it solely as an artistic composition, without regard to the accidental or casual in its surroundings. We must ignore those caressing marks by which we may know that Father Time has passed that way. This added beauty and interest begins where the architect left off; but the latter is too often given the credit for the beauty that is of nature and not of man — the perfect result that neither may obtain alone. The English cathedrals — were they so beautiful, so benign, so satisfying, had they such a pervading aura of spiritual peace when the architect stood off and viewed his finished work, their future history unborn and timid Nature looking askance from afar, not yet ready to run up and cling about the base and storm the walls and find a foothold in every cranny? The architect's work was done even as we see it to-day, but to quicken the observer's pulse something was wanting. There was lacking the subtle human interest which comes from apprenticeship in the service of man. When Goethe spoke of Gothic churches as being " petrified religion " it was to these time-worn veterans that he referred.

Your architect is careful to ignore these aspects of the case, and discounts these pleasant additions to the picture. He prefers the cathedrals of France, though they for the most part stand in the midst of squalid villages whose huts crowd around their base, clinging to the very skirts of Our Lady. These buildings are less appealing, less soft and cajoling, but they stand without extraneous aid to proclaim and attest the great souls and intellects of their creators.

Age has a very potent power of appeal to the sensitive mind.

For time means history, and nothing is more effective in making us feel the presence of the past, in recalling historic events, than buildings which have seen or, perhaps, sheltered them. The power which such works have of revivifying the former life which surged about them, profoundly affecting the imagination of the onlooker by the subtle spirit that permeates them, is a force that must be carefully taken into account and guarded against by him who would sit in judgment on architecture. These pleasant emanations are, for the critic, illegitimate, and must first of all be exorcised before he is fit to don the ermine.

Let us therefore be a little careful in justice to the present-day architect before we are quite sure that our admiration is wisely bestowed, and that our old buildings are really so much finer works than those which are being produced to-day. Let us first try and eliminate Nature and her accessories of verdure and decay; let us try and make allowance for the singularly happy results she obtains by sagging our roofs and staining our walls, by blunting our edges and playing havoc generally with the specifications. It is all very delightful, but it is not architecture. For the same reason, let us banish Father Time from our thoughts, with the rich pageant that follows in his train, and try to discover only what it was that our designer had in his heart, what colored his thoughts, what guided his hand when he stood before his empty field with visions swarming through his brain.

It is a rather singular thing that while we all admire these old buildings and recognize the beauty and charm that is due in such a great measure to age and to what age brings, we are so chary of trying to obtain these results for ourselves, and of trying to get the effect even if we cannot reproduce the cause. For one of their chief charms is the softness of the lines and surfaces. The color due to weathering is harder to get, but there is no reason why we should not try successfully and legitimately to do away with many of our present hard, straight lines, sharp corners and ungracious surfaces. The modern English architects are much

A wider spacing of the timbers marked the later work, after the builder had begun to realize the possibilities of this pliable form of construction

A house at Great Neck, L. I., in which a successful attempt has been made to soften the roof lines

Walker & Hazzard, Architects

further advanced than we in this particular, and it is often impossible to tell the new from the old in their work. They sometimes attain their effects by using old material in order to get the soft, weathered and warm surfaces which they have to offer. It is a common practice to make some farmer happy by giving him a spick-and-span new tile or slate roof in exchange for his old lichen-covered one, or to buy his old brick barn or walls for what to him is a fabulous price for badly worn material, although cheaper for the purchaser than the same materials new. Again, old timber, hand-hewn and lovely with age, is obtained from some old croft, so racked and broken as to be no longer of use as a building. The house shown facing page 50 is a modern house whose air of soft repose is largely owing to its use of old timber. The vertical half-timbers in this case are second-hand railroad sleepers that are, of course, roughly hand-hewn and of indifferent straightness. Spike holes, knots, etc., were not considered anything to be ashamed of, and no elaborate precautions were taken to hide them. The horizontal timbers, which are longer, are bits of old scaffolding; and while it would be easy for the architect to find clients to admire the results, it would be harder to find those who would have the courage to sanction this process. But while these methods are perfectly proper and esthetically legitimate, and should require nothing but courage to employ them, it is a more debatable question when we come to such things as shingle roofs imitating thatch. For in the first case our building is as honest as the day is long, the timbers are as solid and as heavy as they look; they *are* exactly what they *seem*. But what shall we say of these shingle-thatched roofs? The guilty consciences of these builders betray themselves when they hasten to assure us that they are not imitating thatch at all. But when we note the great pains and ingenuity that is lavished on these evidently intractable shingles to make the flat roof curve, the angles blunt, and the roofs melt into one another; when we see the labored inconsequence of the staggering line of shingle butts and the quite startling resemblance to thatch which is the result, it is hard to keep the tongue out of one's cheek. However, it is such a very laudable endeavor to correct the prevailing hardness of outline, and shows such a well developed dissatisfaction in house building à la mode, and is so altogether charming and delightful in the result, that one would be willing to condone a much more serious breach of architectural ethics than this. After all, if "architecture is building that has flowered into beauty," it is well to keep the objective — beauty — more constantly before our eyes and not to be too much occupied in being very sure we are not breaking the rules of design; with the too common result that when we are done, that is all that can be said.

There is an existing confusion due, no doubt, to our Puritan blood, that architecture addresses itself to the moral sense instead of to the eye alone. The idea of a certain school of armchair critics that artistic sincerity and the moral law are identical is one that cannot be buttressed by many of the accepted architectural masterpieces. "'Sincerity,' in many minds, is chiefly associated with speaking the truth; but architectural sincerity is simply obedience to certain visual requirements." To be specific, it is not enough that a column shall be strong enough for its load; it must *look* strong enough.

If Ruskin's observation that "in everything beautiful there is something strange about its proportions," means anything, it means that the humdrum rules have been broken and beauty is the result. Of course it will not do to assume that this is therefore a simple road to architectural success, and that one has only to be lawless to succeed. If one is tempted to think that the rules must then be wrong, the answer is that they are made more to act as watchdogs over the incompetent and to keep bad things from being perpetrated, than to bind those who are capable of producing beauty. The real artist will always rely on instinct and not on rule.

However, we will go more thoroughly into the details of how we may make our houses less hard and cheerless in another place. Suffice it here to know that such results as we see in the old ex-

The timbering and other outside woodwork should be left rough and unpainted

An honest love of simplicity and a healthy scorn for ostentation will rejoice in the possibilities of the modern half-timber house where the half-timbering is used with restraint

amples and which we all admire are not beyond our reach and that what we have come to believe to be the divorce between beauty and utility is in reality but a temporary misunderstanding and not a real case of incompatibility.

These things do not perhaps seem very important to many people, but the fact remains in this curious world that there are those who care tremendously for the fun they can have with their eyes, and who take these matters of beauty and form with inordinate seriousness. We have Oscar Wilde's brilliant biography, in "Pen, Pencil and Poison," of Griffiths Wainewright, the famous dilettante and esthete of the London of the early part of the last century, who combined with his other talents that of a persistent murderer by the use of poison. When this temperamental young man lay in gaol, awaiting transportation for his crimes, he was visited by a friend who reproached him for the wilful murder of his sister-in-law; he shrugged his shoulders and said: "Yes, it was a dreadful thing to do — but she had very thick ankles." It is surprising that some of our sensitive young architects, in a moment of fury against the anatomy of many of our dwellings, are not languishing behind the bars for arson.

We must, however, have an honest love for simplicity and a healthy scorn for ostentation if we are to become happy owners of the type of work of which we have been speaking. It is essentially domestic, cozy, and unmonumental, and if we wish to fertilize envy in our opulent neighbors this is not the way, for our money can be spread out much thinner and the building blown up to twice its size for the same price. We can have Corinthian columns running up through three stories that will outshout our plastered cottage and generally create an impression of fat dividends; for architecture can be made to express coupons as well as slippers and a pipe. We must not fear that "they" will think we build thus because we can afford nothing else. In fact this is not for "them" at all. When Pope Julius II complained because there was no gold on the painted figures of the Sistine

Chapel, " These are simple persons," replied the painter, " simple persons who wore no gold on their garments."

" Half-timber " cannot compete with all gold, and those who have a hankering for the gorgeous will find nothing of interest between these covers.   We are discussing another matter, more homely but closer to the lives of " simple persons."

Another excellent example of the softening influences of time and weather. We cannot hope that a new house will immediately become so much at home in its site

The half-timber house was developed in a flat country and its whole scheme of design was a direct outgrowth of the conditions under which it was evolved. Parenthetically, it is dangerous to employ so much half-timber work on one house

The Choice of Styles

THE half-timber house was developed in a flat country. Its main divisions, its roofing, and all its manifold details, were the direct outgrowth of the conditions under which it was born and had its growth. While it is pos-

Site and Location

sible to build any sort of building anywhere, it is hard to impart to it the appearance which a building should have, of being the only natural and proper building for that particular place. A house should always impress one as being so exactly right that it is almost impossible to imagine any other sort of house in that particular spot. There must be no jar between man's work and Nature's. Each architectural style was developed under different conditions of climate, civilization, materials, requirements and site; and each has its own setting into which it falls perfectly and carries the satisfying conviction, when once it is seen in its right surroundings, that it is inevitably the right thing and fits as perfectly as the last piece in a picture puzzle.

Our English cottages and crofts would look as strange on the rugged hillsides where the Swiss châlet has its home, as the châlet would in the soft, gentle meads of England. Again, the house of the Spanish peasant would never do in England, with its great cornice, thick walls and small windows.

As architecture is the direct outgrowth of conditions and requirements, by fulfilling these conditions, by making straight for the desired goal, following the lines of least resistance, with absolutely no thought of producing " architecture " at all — for art is a result, not a product — we shall in spite of ourselves do just this. Utility and logic are the parents of the " Styles."

The struggle for picturesqueness, in which the various parts of the outside of the building are tortured and twisted to make

a picture, exactly as a painter arranges the objects for his can-
vas, and in which the unwilling plan is dragged hither and yon,

Modern
English
Half-timber
Houses

disjointed, and generally ill used, can only end in
failure. It has been well said that the only artistic
originality worth anything is that which comes from
sincerity. Manufactured picturesqueness results in
a sort of unconscionable stage scenery, and is to
honest work what the landscape of the scenic rail-
way at Coney Island is to nature. It is " scenic " but somehow
does not fill the soul of the nature-lover with a satisfying, solid,
and lasting joy.

We remember that when Gulliver went to Lilliput he found
" a most ingenious architect who had contrived a new method of
building houses, by beginning at the roof and working down-
ward to the foundation, which he justified to me by the practice
of those two prudent insects, the bee and the spider." It would
seem as if this architect must have migrated, to judge by the complicated roofs which we see covering certain houses about us, for
it is hard to believe that their mazy intricacies could have been
achieved by any other method.

We can but repeat what has been said before, that the inside
and outside of a house form an entirety and must not be treated
as two separate things. Picturesqueness is not a success if it
smells of the lamp, and should never be placed first, but as a
welcome addition to the result of logical and straightforward solving of the utilitarian problem. It should be a sort of by-product
of honest building. Picturesqueness is the gay and lovable sister
of Common Sense, who often accompanies her, and over the
result of her cold calculations throws the soft, mysterious veil
of Romance. She appears unheralded before the tired eyes of
the master builder, a timid maid who only comes unsought, and
flees from those who furiously pursue. And so if we find that she
is with us in our excursions, it will be because we are solving our
problems simply and honestly and have forgotten her existence.

It is because each case must be considered by itself that it

is so hard to lay down even general rules of architectural con-
duct, for the exceptional and the normal cases would be about
equal. As we are discussing an English style, let us look at the
sort of house the modern Englishman likes and see how it differs
from the corresponding dwelling in this country.

Before considering the plan in its details let us first try to
come to some understanding of the principles that should operate
in the working out of the problem at hand, no matter what purposes it is called upon to serve.

There are three forms of difficulty in making a good plan,
which are found in varying degrees in individual cases. First:
the plan regarded as a sort of Chinese puzzle in which the object
in view is to arrange the blocks, that is, the rooms, spaces and
conveniences demanded by the owner — all of various shapes,
sizes and uses — so that the best possible result may be obtained,
giving full weight to convenience, comfort and economy of both
space and money. After determining the proper sizes and relation of parts, we shall find the problem resolves itself into a
struggle for compactness, and the elimination of waste space.
Second: we have to consider the plan in relation to architectural composition both within and without. Third: the plan
in its relation to the cost. Of course it is understood that
these difficulties are not to be thought of as being met and overcome all at one time, but on the contrary they are all present in
the mind of the designer from the beginning, and it is a constant
consideration of the varying claims of each — a series of compromises, a sacrificing of the less important for the greater — that
molds the growing work and finally produces the well balanced
result. It is a matter for very nice judgment, for the question
of expenditure, if it is limited, as is usually the case, is a rope that
is continually bringing us up short. Every house would be so
much better if " they " would only spend a little more money!
How to spend the money available to the very best possible advantage is the crux of the matter, and acts as a check to the other
two considerations.

To the disparagement of the architect and to the glory of the owner be it said that the rope is generally lengthened before the end is reached. To the disparagement of the architect, because he should be capable of doing what he is told or of making it known at the start that it is impossible to fulfil the requirements for the given sum. To the glory of the owner, because he comes to recognize before the building is finished that he is spending more money than he ever spent before in his life, that he has demanded so much in the first place and has caused his money to be spread so thin, that the quality is bound to suffer not only in the materials and workmanship but in a baldness that transcends simplicity. There is danger of all the work being inadequate unless he adds a little more. In other words, the difference between having everything half right and exactly right is not very great, and he very sensibly finishes properly what he has begun.

But we may now reverse the epithets. It is to the disparagement of the owner that he is so seldom frank with his architect and so seldom means what he says. Perhaps it is because he has heard that architects always exceed the stipulated cost and so he thinks that by naming some sum below what he is really prepared to pay he will be clever enough to gain his ends and diplomatic enough not to hurt the architect's feelings. Perhaps he has read in the " Marvellous Wisdom and Quaint Conceits," of Thomas Fuller, writing in the seventeenth century, that "In building rather believe any man than an artificier . . . should they tell thee all the cost at the first, it would blast a young builder at the budding." If this is the reason it is a great mistake, because it leads to the design of a scheme for the house with the low cost in view, and when toward the end the owner begins to show a disposition to spend more and have things better it is too late for additions. There is no outlet, except for such things as beamed ceilings, paneling in rooms not designed for it, better toilet fixtures in the too small bathrooms, extra rooms forced into an attic planned for nothing but storage, or more plumbing poorly accom-

A delightful little gardener's house in a congenial setting at Waltham, Mass.

John A. Frye, Architect

Cope & Stewardson, Architects

A house at Princeton, N. J.   The English character would have been enhanced had the first story been built of something other than stone

modated in out-of-the-way places. Often, however, the owner
cannot be accused of disingenuousness in stating his intentions;
perhaps more often he makes it a cast iron condition at the start
that he *must* have certain things and that he will *not* pay but a
given sum. It is not hard to see that these two fiats on his part
are seldom a good fit, and that it is the demands that are usually
too large to cram into the sum. Then, he being adamant for
both, it usually ends in his having what he wants and paying
for it.

And to continue and justify our classification, it is to the glory
of the architect that he is often able to find the hidden truth of
the whole matter of which even the owner is unconscious, and so
save the owner from himself. The course of education which the
owner of a new house has forced upon him is appalling, as he is
the first to recognize when he looks back over the finished work.
If at the start he is sometimes inclined to the idea that it is all
a matter that he, a strong man, can take by the throat, he usually
ends in a more chastened frame of mind, and with greater respect
for building problems. The architect is tempted to paraphrase
the witty French woman who said, " Men are different but all
husbands are alike," and say that " Men are different but all
clients are alike."

Now that we have considered some of the lions in the path
leading to our castle in the air, and how they are to be tamed or
circumvented, let us consider what is the desideratum in a home
after all, and how we may obtain it. It may be taken almost as
an axiom that the same problem never occurs twice. It has been
calculated that the chances of a man's emptying a basket full of
letters off the roof of a house and having them form themselves
into Homer's Iliad on the lawn, is quite remote. The chances
are about the same of there ever being two exactly similar families
of exactly similar wealth, who desire to spend the same fraction
of it for exactly the same house in size, arrangement, and appearance, on duplicate pieces of land and surroundings. " There
ain't no such animal," as the farmer said when he saw the hippo-

potamus. Every architect knows how impossible it is ever to use the same plan twice, and for this reason books of ready-made plans can never offer a real fit in any case, and are pernicious in their paper plausibility divorced from the site and its orientation.

English and American House Plans

THE two accompanying plans have been selected as examples of moderate-priced English country houses of the sort that are built and lived in to-day by the well-to-do classes. They are not given because they are particularly good or particularly bad, but as plans that possess features typical of present-day work and commonly found in the average house inhabited by the cultivated British family. They are instructive because, being modern houses and planned to suit the occupant, they throw an interesting light on the demands and predilections of the English. They are instructive because they give a glimpse of English character, and their difference from houses of a similar class in this country is a measure of a true ethnological difference in the peoples, which is more subtly expressed in bricks and mortar than it would be possible to do it in words. Here we have a sermon in stones. We shall see that the desire for privacy with our British cousins is almost morbid, and is equalled only by the desire for coziness and the hatred of formality and stiffness. This makes itself felt in the strict eschewing of symmetry or axes in the plan, or anything that tends to formality. The American desire for a " house that opens up well " would be inconceivable to them. Their walled gardens, rooms with small doors, each cut off from the others, low ceilings and love of fireplace and inglenook, all speak of the desire for informal domestic life and slippered ease.

Let us now look at the first of these plans. One of the most prominent of contemporary English architects in writing of this plan says, " The site was quite without any sense of privacy, in the residential part of the town. An attempt has been made to remedy this in the irregular form of building and the arched entry to the forecourt." To an American, fifty feet from the road " in the residential part of the town " would in itself have answered all the demands of privacy; instead of further putting a hedge

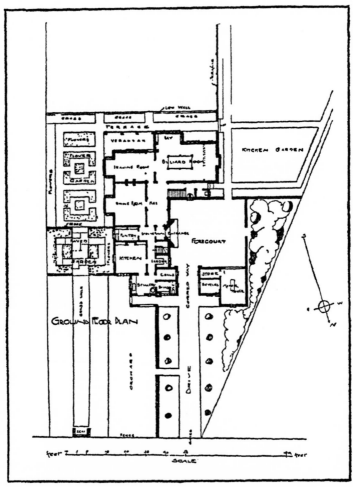

The plan of a modern English home, selected at random, illustrating the Englishman's insistence upon seclusion

between him and the street he would infallibly have tried to get back into things by building a great piazza across the entire front of the house. But this very typical Briton, after he has retreated thus far, throws his scullery and garage up in front of

the master's portion of the house as a guard, and drives under
a portcullis-like entrance to an entirely enclosed court where he
may get out of his carriage in reasonable safety from being seen
— this was built before flying machines, and the chance of being
discovered now being enormously increased, he will doubtless
roof his court.   So far, then, having fought the good fight against
the distressing publicity of his plot of land, let us suppose that
by hook or crook, bribery and corruption we have penetrated

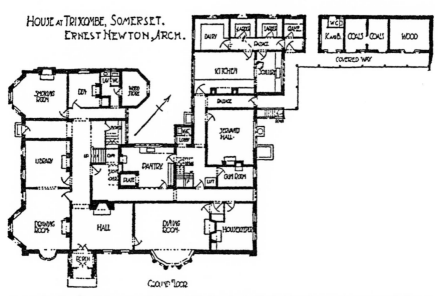

It worries the Englishman and his architect not at all that in the service from kitchen to
dining-room the maids must traverse the full depth of the house

into the forecourt.   It is of good size and almost entirely surrounded by the wings of the house, the effect being very charming and interesting.   We see that the building covers a great deal
of ground and we stand before the great door in the centre of the
main house with lively expectation of what will burst upon us
when the butler flings open the door.   When the door is opened
we see stretching ahead of us — the " pantry "!   Hastily turning
to the right and pretending we have n't noticed, we enter a fair-
sized hall from which suspicious little doors allow us grudgingly

to enter what are sure to be delightful rooms. The stairs we discover later have scudded around the corner and are hiding in the darkest end of the hall.

If the greeting offered to the stranger by this typical arrangement seems lacking in effusive and expansive cordiality, have we not heard the same charge brought against its typical owner?

One of the strange features of English house-planning which is better seen in the second plan is the distance and general lack

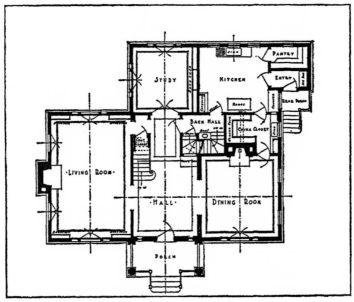

A typical plan for an American home that " opens up well "

of connection between the kitchen and dining-room. It is more common than not for the butler to have to walk some distance past the front door or through a corridor used by the household to reach the dining-table. It may be of value to the tardy dresser to be reminded that dinner is waiting by the odor of the cauliflower as it is borne through the house; and to have to stand aside to let one's soup pass would at least give us useful advance knowledge which might make up for some loss of heat. This tells us very plainly that it is unnecessary to make it easy for servants where they are so plentiful and so good; the designs of our houses in this country are too often sacrificed to make snares to keep them.

Now let us return to the United States and consider what we have taken as a typical suburban plan as we see it in its essentials. It is placed not too far from the street, the main living-rooms facing it and a piazza big or little about the front door which is often located in the middle. This brings the hall in the centre of the house and we have at once on entering a perfect view of the rooms on either side through *large* doors, usually sliding or folding. Every nook and corner is exposed. One may rake the whole master's portion at a glance. No reticence here, no secrets — you are taken into the heart of the home at once, and unless you are a modest man and swerve from your path, you will find yourself walking upstairs into the boudoir. This is indeed a "house that opens up well"; it is "good for entertaining," fine circulation, light, sun and air. I think it must be that we have a feeling that it is snobbish and unfriendly, perhaps a trifle undemocratic — that bogey and knock-down argument in the arsenal of every freeborn American — to wall one's garden or sit away from the traffic, or pull down one's curtain. We do not feel the need of privacy ourselves, and the existence of the feeling in others would rob us of a great deal that is intensely interesting. Walls, or being away from the street make it difficult to see the passing. It is hard not to know what the neighbors are doing.

It is not a matter that is at all related to expense; when our plodder in the ranks has received his captain's stripes, we shall find his half-million-dollar house is fundamentally the same. He does not build a big, comfortable mansion house with much thought to the stable, kennels, grounds and other appurtenances of a country gentleman. Instead of such a house he builds an enormous palace, cold, formal and sumptuous. Planned on axes, we still see on entering the door, virtually the whole. That the slightly bewildered owner feels somewhat awed in the presence of so much monumental dignity is betrayed by the insertion, in some out-of-the-way corner, of a small office where he and his battered roll-top desk may metaphorically fall into each other's arms; here he will make himself a little home within a home. We love to dwell on our open plumbing and patent thermostats and electric curling irons, and say that the poor Englishman does n't know what comfort is. No mistake can be greater. He cares so much for his comfort, he so wants what he wants as he wants it, that he will let *nothing* stand in his way — nothing else is important. He will sacrifice trying to impress his neighbors by external pretentiousness, he will let no architectural consideration rob him of his privacy and coziness. His entertainments will have to do the best they can; he has figured out that he entertains a few times in a year and lives in his house every day. He surrounds himself with his horses and dogs and motor cars, the keynote of comfort is well sustained in the milieu that he loves to make for himself, and the life that goes on in his little group of buildings is almost as complete and diverse as that under the roof of a medieval monastery.

So much for the differences that are cardinal and indigenous in the English work. When Charles Dudley Warner said that he would as lief have an Englishman without side whiskers, he might have been just as forceful if he had said that he would just as lief have an Englishman who did n't live in a cottage.

Let us consider these houses in relation to our own, and see if there are not some valuable lessons to be learned from them.

A modern half-timber house at Essex Fells, N. J., with the typical
diagonal end-braces and greater elaboration in the bays

Close observation of the English work will help us to avoid the tendency toward too great elaboration in the timber patterns

How to Plan the House

WHATEVER we shall have to say under this caption regarding the plan of the house and its arrangements, must of necessity be in many ways as applicable in all essentials to houses of other styles as to half-timber houses. While there are certain arrangements that are typical of the particular kind of house of which we are writing — a certain freedom of design which we like to think is not always obtainable when the plan must be wedded to a more exacting exterior expression, it is nevertheless true that for utilitarian reasons such as the elimination of waste motion, and for the general convenience of living under the conditions of modern civilization, our houses must very closely reflect our lives. *Laissez faire* is not a motto for a restless and progressive race. Emerson's comment when he heard that Margaret Fuller had said that she " had decided to accept the world as she found it " is still the voice of wisdom. He said, " She 'd better! " And so, if we decide to accept motor cars and babies, vacuum cleaners and regular meals, books and the gregarious theory of man, we shall all have something in common in starting to build a shelter.

We hope it will be a half-timber shelter, but in any case there are bound to be certain necessary rooms, and their functions we shall find automatically determining their relations with one another. What further rooms or space we may add over and above what may be termed necessities will be a matter of individual preference and mode of living. In the discussion that follows the author has had more in mind the usages and mode of life in this country than in England, where half-timber work has its home, but the general character of its plan, its untrammeled irregularities, its silhouette, as it were; the spaces to be walled and roofed, will be much alike in either case.

In the first place it is often true that on a given piece of ground there may be several spots where it is perfectly possible to build an economical, attractive and livable house, and personal taste and individual predilections should be carefully consulted before reaching a decision. The general scheme and size of the building must not be lost sight of for a moment, and the question of the fit of the house on the land should be very carefully gone into and with as little left to guesswork and approximation as possible. The grade of the land, if the piece is sloping, is a most deceptive thing, and always tends to look more nearly level than is actually the case. It is an excellent plan in considering any given spot to do a little rough leveling. A small level will do very well, and even a bottle almost entirely full with its little air bubble has been known to give satisfactory results. When we have to deal with a piece of land other than a city lot, it is often a problem how we shall face the house, or whether the orientation shall be governed by the sun or by the view. In any case, before we draw our plans we should have a topographical map made of so much of the grounds as we propose to deal with, giving two-foot elevation lines if the piece is large and the ground very rough, or one-foot lines if there is less difficulty. It is folly to attempt to do serious, careful work without knowing accurately the levels to be encountered. Curiously enough the southern aspect in the old English house was often purposely avoided. Andrew Baard, the health faddist of the sixteenth century, instructs those who build to:

"Ordre and edyfy the house so that the pryncipale and chief prospects may be eest and west, specially north eest; south eest and south west for the meryal of al wyndes is the most worste, for the south wynde doth corrupt and doth make eyyll vapours. The eest wynde is temperate, fryske, and fragrant. The west wind is mutable; the north wynde purgeth yll vapours; wherefore better it is of the two worste that the windows do open playne north than playne south."

Now while it is not likely that the characters of these

" wyndes " have changed much since these observations, it at least would seem that those who " ordre and edyfy " the house have somewhat changed their minds about what they like. In this country, at least, those who dwell near the Atlantic seaboard will acknowledge that while the " eest wynde is fryske " they may be less ready to assent to the idea that the southwest is the " most worste."

For houses that are to be exclusively for summer use in a section of the country where the heat is not a thing to be avoided, it is naturally the view which will have preference in the lay-out of the principal living-rooms. However, in houses that are to be lived in all the year round it is rarely good policy to ignore the cheerful track of Old Sol, and it is a remarkable view indeed that would justify us in placing our living-room where the sun would not enter during a considerable part of the day.

Having placed our living-room, we have next to determine the relative positions of the dining-room and hall. For the dining-room we shall be wise to try for either an east, northeast or southeast corner so that we may have the sun at breakfast with its powerful aid to cheerfulness at this depressing period of the day. Whether it may not be wise to still further dispel the natural gloom by adding a fireplace is a fair question. Unless, however, the dining-room is a large one, some one is sure to have too warm a back, as with a dining-table in the centre the seats of those about it are bound to be close to the four walls. A fireplace may, however, often be economically placed in this room as it will probably be near enough to the kitchen to have one of its chimney flues, placed there for that purpose, used for the kitchen range, the smoke pipe from which may be easily made to pass through an intervening butler's pantry or some service space of the sort. Again as a further antidote for the blues, a window bay for flowers is a welcome addition, and the morning sun will make the arrangement an eminently practical one.

The dining-room fixed, we have not so much latitude in placing the kitchen, as in this country it is an almost universal custom, having as its reason economy of steps and time, to have it next the dining-room, or at least separated from it only by the butler's pantry through which it may be entered, or else by means of a short hall out of which the pantry leads. It is very desirable that there shall be two doors between these rooms, to shut out the noise and the odors that tend to penetrate from the kitchen to the dining-room, and the butler's pantry makes a very welcome buffer between the two. If the dining-room is on the southeast this may well bring the kitchen on the northwest. This is the least desirable corner of the house for other rooms, and not at all objectionable for the purposes to which a kitchen is put. It is the coldest corner of the house, and as the kitchen is apt to be the hottest room, rather hotter than those who work there desire, it is well that it should stand as a protector and advance guard against the chill north winds. Also the pantry or larder, which will be near-by, is the one room in the house that should never see the sun, and the same is true of the neighboring shed where the refrigerator has its place. The placing of the front door and hall are governed by both the position of the living-room and the location of the street. While it is most often found on the front of the house, there is no reason why it should not be on either side if it will help in the placing of our other rooms where we want them. In small work we shall do well to make up our minds to saving space in the hall and using it to better advantage elsewhere. After the stairs are arranged all we shall need is room enough for a chest, a chair or two and space enough to speed the parting guest.

This disposes of the essential parts of the ordinary house of moderate cost. There are various rooms that are very commonly added to this skeleton and which in individual cases are considered essential, although they are not really fundamental and should properly be considered as luxurious and delightful additions of which we shall have as many as we can afford. It is a question whether the vestibule should come under the head of a necessity or a luxury. If the door is on the northwest and is unprotected

H. Baillie Scott, Architect

"The Hall," Seal Hollow, Sevenoaks, Kent, England. The end wall shows
brick filling between the timbers

The dining-room of a modern American house in which the spirit of the old work has been caught

Frederick J. Sterner, Architect

by a porch and the house situated in a cold climate, it is perhaps a necessity. It is apt to be a nuisance if it is too small, the maid having to flatten herself behind the door on one side while the visitor squirms by on the other.

The library should be one of the most attractive rooms in the house, and it is not difficult to make it so. It is not necessary for one to be of such a literary turn as to say with Seigneur Montaigne of his library, " There is my seat, there is my throne. There without order and without method — by piece meales — I turn over and ransacke nowe one book and now another . . . and walking up and down I endight and register these my humors, these my conceits. There I pass the greatest part of my live days, and weare out most hours of the day." The library will be situated near the living-room but should always be slightly withdrawn from the bustle and general life of both it and the entrance hall; and this whether it partakes more of the character of a real study, where the master of the house has work to do, or of that type of room which the mild-mannered commuter loves to refer to by the savage title of " Den." Sanctum is another name for this room that is nowadays perhaps a little out of fashion. If he is even more businesslike he may call it an office. They are all different names for the master's room, and the " library " is only the aristocrat of the lot. Any room that can be filled with books is *ipso facto* a success. They are perfectly capable of taking the job out of the hands of the interior decorator and making a success of it without the slightest strain or effort. If the owner is able to sheathe his walls with well filled, or perhaps one might better say *entirely* filled bookcases — and for decorative purposes the back of Laura Jean Libby is on a par with that of Meredith — he is a fortunate man and will have a more splendid wall covering than any decorator can sell him. But he will destroy what he has so well begun if he allows any meticulous housewife to induce him to hang glass doors in front of his shelves. The high lights and reflections from the panes will be a jarring note, and the whole effect clumsy and mercantile. The shelves should be on movable pegs so as to be adjusted to any height and sheathed at the back, and may well have a row of drawers next the floor somewhat deeper than the shelves, for magazines, games, etc., the extra depth giving a shelf on top for which one will find plenty of uses. The bookcases will be built-in, and only as a last resort, or in a strictly business library, should the sectional bookcase be resorted to. It may have a great future, but its past and present are deplorable. If to the wall of parti-colored bindings he adds a fireplace, not forgetting to build into the side of the breast a cupboard of ample size to hold the necessary lubricants to free and comfortable male intercourse, the cheery blaze will complete the picture.

The reception room was formerly felt to be an unerring mark of respectability, and was demanded in the smallest houses even if it took half the space that might have gone into the living-room. This feeling has rather had its day among the average builders of ten- to fourteen-room houses. Its omission is a real step in advance, resulting not only in a simpler form of hospitality, much more fitting for those concerned, but is a distinct architectural aid to the rest of the plan of the house. Formerly, when working with a limited amount of floor space at one's disposal (for floor space and money are equivalents), and the problem called for a reception room, it was bound to mean that the dining-room, hall, and the living-room suffered. It was just as plain that the other three rooms must be smaller with its introduction, as it is that quarters are less than thirds. Instead of three good rooms we had four bad ones, whereas now by giving this space to the living-room we may have a fine big room, the inertia of whose ample space expands the soul and soothes the nerves. For a big, generous room has psychotherapeutic value as well as its more obvious physical advantages. An old book on building speaks of the reception room as a "Chamber of Delight." We are inclined to think that it must be a very, very old book indeed, as that is not a good description of the modern affair. The reception room nowadays is too often a tawdry foster-child of the honest home, its meretricious elegance having nothing in common with the rest of the house or its inhabitants; as a sophisticated, citified, lineal descendant of the chill country parlor with its wax flowers and gilt copy of Miss Hemans' poems, it is passing away. *Requiescat in pace.* Not that we are to understand that a reception room is always a mistake, for when the size of the house and the general style of living warrant it, it is as indispensable as the library. We only wish to plead with the small house against putting on airs and squandering precious space so unwisely.

The sun parlor or morning-room is considered a necessity by the English but is not often found with us. In the country house it bears much the same relation to the living-room that the breakfast room does to the dining-room. It is a room for pipes and sewing, and will let onto a terrace with the garden not far off and the flowers peering in. It is the sort of room in which the dog may fittingly doze in the sun, where all the chairs should have arms so that we may hang our legs over them, and where sewing threads really look well on the floor. A delightful room for novels and tea and flirting, or for anything, for that matter, that is not weighty or portentous. In California, where house heating takes the form of going outdoors to get warm, the sun parlor fills a real need, and to live in the sun under glass like a Hamburg grape is a most comfortable experience.

The billiard room, which in England is often found on the first floor near the other living-rooms, is in this country more often relegated to the basement or attic; when so done, however, it is usually because of lack of space elsewhere. The billiard room being strictly for business — the business of play — need have little attention to outlook or the points of the compass. The essential thing is plenty of light and adequate size; it should not be less than fifteen feet by eighteen feet, and should be larger to accommodate seated spectators. A fireplace is a welcome addition in any case, as the room is apt to partake of the functions of a lounging-room, and heat in some way should be provided. It is ruinous to ivory balls to let them become too cold.

If we were in an English half-timber house we should consider the " gun room " under this head, but as this is not an ordinary requirement in this country we need not let it detain us further than to say that if we require such a private arsenal it would naturally take its place along with the library and billiard room.

The coat closet, which there is a growing tendency to amplify and expand into a lavatory or brush room, is best situated near the front door and generally off the front hall, where those entering the house may at once repair and wash and brush up and leave their wraps, before entering the house proper, where they may then meet the owner on his own footing. It is an excellent arrangement also where there are children, and may well serve as a barrier against further inroads of rubber boots and dirty hands. We are somewhat hampered the moment we introduce plumbing into a room or closet of this sort by the necessity of direct ventilation, which means an outside window. This is compulsory under the laws of many cities and towns, and is a rule that should be observed whether or not officially promulgated. Although the science of sanitary plumbing has made almost revolutionary strides in the past two decades and is now both in theory and execution almost perfection, it has not, and probably never will, arrive at a point where it is hygienically advisable to dispense with direct outside ventilation for the water-closet.

The next addition we shall probably make will be a breakfast room. This is a most useful and pleasant room in a large house where the dining-room will probably be a room of some size and dignity, the sort of room with which we are quite *en rapport* at a brilliant dinner party, an excellent background, with its stately splendor, to the subdued gaiety of the occasion. A room of this character, however, is apt to look in the clear virgin light of eight o'clock in the morning like the traditional " banquet hall deserted," and is a fit companion only for one who has dined

Too few of us are willing to stand by our convictions and use old material in a new house. Mr. C. Harrison Townsend has utilized old railroad sleepers for the vertical timbers in this house in Surrey, England

Modern English houses at Port Sunlight, one of the model English villages

there the night before and appears next morning in the gay habiliments of the feast.   To be frank, we must acknowledge that our splendid dining-room makes a depressing breakfast room.   The austerity of heavy silver and mahogany act as a rebuke to our obvious let-down from our gracious dignity of the night before. We are uneasy and irritated in its presence; we are discovered and feel no better than hypocrites, and are in no mood to be lectured over the eggs and bacon.   It is this feeling almost of necessity that has been the mother of the invention of the breakfast room.   It may either take the form of an alcove leading off the main dining-room, or it may be, that, following the lines of least resistance, it will develop into a separate room; in either case it will not be far from the dining-room as they must both be within easy reach of the butler's pantry and kitchen.   The points to be insisted upon in regard to it are that it shall have plenty of morning sun, that it must not be too large, and that its furniture and decorations strike the light and cheerful note.   If dignified and splendid are suitable words for the dining-room, pretty and cozy should describe its offspring.   Tints should take the place of decided colors; hangings, rugs and upholstery should take on a playful and frivolous character.

It is very common in the English half-timber houses and is even more appropriate in this country, to have a terrace somewhere adjoining the house, and it is a very happy arrangement if it includes the dining-room.   It is very pleasant in summer to have this foreground to the garden view beyond, and to have one's meals *al fresco* is most delightful.   Here we have a dining-room indeed with the welkin for our ceiling and walls of jocund posies.   We may be as practical as we like, screen it in and cover it with a roof — if we are not on easy terms of familiarity with all outdoors — or we may compromise with a less solid form of shelter, such as an awning of more or less temporary kind, or better still with vines on some informal arrangement of poles and crossbars supported on posts.   We are trying hard to avoid the word "pergola."   The chairs and tables should be of the sort that can be left out in all weather. Practical convenience will be served if it can be planned to have a window in the butler's pantry to be used as a slide by the maid in serving and clearing away, particularly when rain appears uninvited to the feast, as is sometimes the case, and the adjournment must be done in a hurry!

The modern contrivance of a conservatory is a delightful addition, that, with our modern heating appliances, is not so great an extravagance as the name conveys to the minds of most people. The construction may vary in elegance all the way from what a handy man around the house will make in his spare time with window sash, to the very elegant and quasi-oriental structure that the professional greenhouse men will erect. The size must be carefully considered and we must not, in the enthusiasm of the moment, build too large, for while one cannot have too many flowers one can easily find them too much care. Old Thomas Fuller in " The Holy State " gives us seven maxims, the last bit of wisdom being, " A house had better be too little for a day than too great for a year." Whether he was living in a greenhouse when he threw this stone we do not know, but at any rate it was sufficiently well aimed.

The conservatory may be connected with the house but should not be a part of it. It should have its own heating plant, which should be either a steam or hot-water system. The hot air from a furnace is too dry, no matter what precautions are taken, for the best growth of plants. The moisture and temperature which the inhabitants of the greenhouse require will be too much for the inhabitants of the house, and for this reason the two should be separated. A conservatory letting off the dining-room is a favorite location, but its placing will be governed by so many things peculiar to each individual plan that it is of little use to try to lay down rules. It is sometimes arranged to glass-in part of a covered piazza using adjustable heating pipes to put it up and take it down with the seasons. This is a sensible thing to do when the amount of space is limited. The floor should be either of tile, brick, cement, or the ground itself, and properly drained to carry off surface water. It should never be of wood.

Coming to the service portion of the house, we shall find that an enormous amount of time and ingenuity has been expended in improving the infinite number of things that go to minister more or less directly to the ease and comfort of the other end of the house. We sometimes have a suspicion that the desire for convenience overleaps itself and the results become so complex as to offset with their intricacies what they gain. It is often a very pretty question with these ingenious labor-saving devices whether in the hurlyburly of daily use they are worth the bother. However, such things as plate slides, ash chutes from the fire-box to the ash barrel, gas hot-water heaters, gas and electric ranges, vacuum cleaners, clothes chutes, etc., seem to have proved their worth and to have come to stay. To the bare skeleton of kitchen, pantry and china-closet — for which " butler's pantry " is a more descriptive name, even though it is tacitly understood that it will never see its titular owner — we may articulate a servants' hall, laundry, shed, cold room, coal bins, toilet room, closets, etc., all of which will be very welcome to those who work here.

Just a word about the kitchen before we leave it. In the first place, all women may be divided into two classes: those who believe in large kitchens and those who favor small ones. A small one will measure about ten by twelve feet; anything smaller than this is really a kitchenette. The advocates of a small kitchen talk of having everything handy and of saving steps. The arguments for a large kitchen are plenty of elbow room and light and air. In either case it is desirable to have the windows large, placed near the ceiling, and so arranged as to give a cross draught. The placing of tables and sinks in the centre of the room, which is popular in England, is only possible in a large kitchen, and even there the complaint is made that one is continually having to walk around them. A hood should be placed over the range, ventilated into a special flue alongside of, or in the centre of, the hot range flue; making it a warm flue insures a pulling draught which will do wonders towards taking off the hot air and odors as they rise from the cooking. There should be a dresser for table china, etc., if there is to be no servants' dining-room, and space for a table. The floor may be cork tile, which is the best, or wood, composition, linoleum or tile. This latter works well and is easily cleaned but is hard on the feet. Wood floors are difficult to keep looking well, and no surface finish will last, no matter what the advertisement says. The various compositions in the market are good, but are likely to crack over a wood floor.

The laundry will be the first addition, and it is no longer considered a luxury to have this a separate room, either near the kitchen or more often in the basement beneath the kitchen. When so located great care must be taken to be sure that it is provided with plenty of light. The ordinary cellar window will not do. It is usually placed under the kitchen so that the kitchen plumbing and chimney may be utilized. It should also have easy access to the cellar door and clothes-yard without, and should of course be provided with artificial light. If there is no wood floor but only cement, it will be well to have a wood grille in front of the tubs for the workers to stand on, thus keeping their feet dry and off the cold cement.

The servants' dining-room, or, as they say in England, the " servants' hall," is a practical necessity when there are more than two servants who take their meals in the house. Their presence in the kitchen, even if it is a large one, is a constant source of annoyance and irritation to the cook, and the number of square feet that it would be necessary to add to the size of the kitchen for their accommodation would much better be set aside as a separate room. It will serve as a dining-room with a dresser for the accommodation of the necessary table ware, and as a sitting-room when they are off duty. It may be quite small but should be close to the kitchen so as to minimize the labor of serving the meals and washing up afterwards. Sometimes an alcove is made off the kitchen, but this takes as much space as a separate room and is not nearly so satisfactory from any point of view, particularly when there are men to be fed. It is very desirable to keep them out of the kitchen.

A shed, which is considered an absolute necessity in the country, will be hailed with delight anywhere. Its uses are manifold and cannot be catalogued. It is a sort of refuge for outcasts that cannot claim a more definite residence. They will be a diverse and motley company to be sure, these waifs: the velocipede with its pedals looks with pity on the one-armed ice-cream freezer; the ironing-board will gaze with padded contempt on the naked mahogany table leaves; while an assortment of garden tools will modestly seek to hide behind a bristling rubbish barrel; and king over all is the portly refrigerator. This last, however, is often placed in a small recess in the back vestibule, just large enough to receive it, between the outside back door to the porch and the one to the kitchen. Again, an excellent arrangement is to have it in the pantry, provided it is not too near the kitchen range, and the ice may be put through a door in the wall, either from a back hall or from outside the house. This latter method is very popular as it keeps the iceman entirely out of the house, which is just as well as he has been known to hit on the bright idea that slipping an egg or two into his pocket will help moderate the high cost of living! He must at any rate be kept out of the kitchen, with his dripping ice and muddy boots. Refrigerators are now made with ice doors built into the back. In large establishments the refrigerator may assume a more commodious form and become a cold room all by itself. This is a small insulated room entered by a tight-fitting door with a great trough for ice on the outside wall, the ice being fed in through a high door in the back, the walls supporting shelves, hooks, etc., for the food.

We must be sure to find a corner somewhere — it need not be large — that can be turned into a closet for brooms, mops, etc., and which may also serve as a coat closet. The omission of this small affair causes an amount of feeling that is surprising, and it is hard to realize, if we may believe our ears, that it is not quite the most important affair in the house.

Our pantry must have an outside window so that we may keep it cool, and for the same reason it must be located where the sun will enter as little as possible — never, if it can be arranged. It must have cupboards for flour and sugar barrels, crocks, etc., a few drawers with a wide counter under the window, a mixing-board of plate glass or a marble slab, and plenty of open shelf room. Part of these shelves may well be protected from flies by being partitioned off with a screened door.

There is a tendency to make kitchen pantries too large, just as there is a tendency to make butlers' pantries too small. The latter should contain a two-part sink of German silver if possible, with the metal brought up to cover the counter and run up six inches on the walls. If its cost puts this out of the question we must make a tinned-copper-lined box sink do, the objection to this being that the tin plating soon wears off and allows the copper to show through. Iron or porcelain sinks are not good here as they are apt to crack the china. The chance of getting a cupboard under the sink should not induce us to enclose this space. The plumbing pipes and trap should, for sanitary reasons, be left open to the air.

We should see to it that we have two banks of drawers, the bottom one deep enough for table linen and long enough for centre-pieces. The top drawers should be shallow, say four inches deep, divided by slender partitions, and lined with felt for silver. We must get all the counterspace and glazed cupboards with shelves to the ceiling that are possible. Our cupboard doors may either be hinged to swing, or slide on tracks. The objection to the hinged door is that if it is left open by any chance it hangs out into the passage and will cause trouble as an obstacle in the dark, or when the maid is intent on her work. The sliding doors for this reason are probably better, though they have been known to stick, and as their being left open carries no penalty with it, we shall find in practice that this is too often the case.

Beneath our counter, in addition to our drawers, we may have cupboards, a safe, and perhaps a small refrigerator for salads, desserts and such things, and a plate-warmer. This latter often takes the form of a small radiator designed for the purpose. This of course can be done only when the house is heated by hot water or steam, and even then will be useless when our winter heat is discontinued. Gas is also used. The electric plate-warmer is perhaps the best; the objection that it may be left turned on can be overcome by placing a red light on the same circuit, which will show in the pantry or kitchen, and act as a reminder. This may also be done with the cellar light which we sometimes forget to turn off when the switch is at the head of the stair. We should have a slide at the level of the counter, opening into the kitchen, and the counter should be continuous if possible so that dishes may be slid right through from pantry to kitchen. Our table leaves may also find a specially designed home here, and such conveniences as towel racks, sliding counter extensions, platter racks, drop shelves, disappearing steps for the top shelves, etc., will all or many of them find a place.

The distance of the front hall from the kitchen should be as direct and short as possible, and, it is hardly necessary to add, should avoid taking us through any room. On the other hand, the kitchen should be cut off from the front hall and the master's portion by at least two doors, which will necessarily mean some sort of hall or closet between, giving us the dead air space which is so desirable for sound-proofing and as a protection against the kitchen odors. Doors occupying such strategic points as these should not be relied upon to keep their openings closed unaided, and a substantial automatic door check will be found to have a much better memory than the best trained maid, and at the same time will prevent the possibility of slamming either from draughts or other causes. It will often be found convenient, in small houses, to glorify this passage by a slight expansion into a coat closet and telephone booth, and it may even be found possible to have the cellar stairs go down out of it, of course with a door at the top. It may also be found advisable to have the back stairs go up from it.

The exigencies of the more important rooms will probably have forced this hall into the interior of the house, and it will in that case be necessary to borrow light from the butler's pantry or kitchen through a sash in the wall, or to insert a light of glass in one of the doors. If this proves to be the case we should resolutely give up any ideas of introducing a water-closet into this space.

It is better not to have either the cellar stairs or the back stairs to the second floor lead directly out of the kitchen, even with a door to cut them off at the start. Odors and dampness never seem content to stay where they happen to be, and may be relied upon to break through and start on their wanderings through these convenient passageways. This matter of the small interior hall is not of course an ideal arrangement and will be resorted to only in very small work where space must be very economically apportioned. This is the principle of the relation of the kitchen and the front hall reduced to its lowest terms. In bigger work we shall avoid enclosed space without outside air or light, and generally increase and amplify the connecting links.

Arriving in the front hall, we are now back where we started and ready to go to the second floor.

Before leaving the ground floor we might say a few words of a general nature regarding some of the common problems that often have to be decided in the arrangement of the main living-rooms. If we are building on a site which is of a naturally irregular surface with considerable change of grade over that portion where our house is to stand, it is a perfectly natural and sensible thing to fit the house to the ground as much as may be, by lowering or raising the floor level with the changes of the grade, thus not only effecting an economy of material but fitting the building to its site. Our reward will be that only true and satisfying picturesqueness which is the result of meeting logically and naturally, in the most direct way, the problem as one finds it.

We must, however, be careful in planning not to let such

The plan of the half-timber house, by reason of its pliability, may provide, as here,
for incorporating the garage into one end of the building

The garage is incorporated into the service end of the house, thereby incidentally avoiding the discomforts of a cold work-room and the freezing of water in the car's radiator

changes of level occur in locations which will interfere with the ease of carrying on the work of the household. The shifting of a step a few feet will often make a vast difference; for instance from one side of a door to the other, to form part of a neighboring run of steps, and so on. If changes of level occur in the middle of a room it has the practical effect of dividing it into two distinct rooms and where we had one big room before we shall have the equivalent of two small ones. If one is on the upper level in a room so divided he will always be haunted by the fear that he may forget and step backwards. It will be forcing on him an added responsibility which he will unconsciously resent. We must also be careful not to place steps where they are not to be expected or where they will be badly lighted, or we shall have accidents. When only two or three steps occur they must be made wider and much more ample than is at all necessary in a long flight.

The matter of a fireplace is always a vital one and if we are to have a chimney it is often a temptation to locate it so that it will serve two or more rooms. This of course is an economy if it does not result in our having two fireplaces where we do not want them, instead of one where we do. For instance, if we have a living-room and library adjoining, we are often tempted to put a chimney in the partition between with fireplaces in each room, back to back. More often than not, however, this will bring them close to the entrance doors, which is not a good arrangement, not only because of the draught but because it will prevent a drawing of chairs about the fire. And fully equal to these real inconveniences is the instinctive feeling that there is a lack of coziness. One never saw a cat pick out a spot to sleep in between a door and a fireplace.

There are some people who so object to stairs that they endeavor to have as much of the house as possible on the first floor. The pros and cons of a ground-floor bedroom are sufficiently obvious, and it resolves itself into a matter of personal taste. There is no sound reason for not having one's sleeping-room on the ground floor. Those who don't like it give as a reason — that they don't like it! It seems to be another case of

"I do not like you, Dr. Fell,
The reason why I cannot tell,
But this at least I know full well,
I do not like you, Dr. Fell."

Which is often the best of reasons because it is so impervious to argument.

Lest you, gentle reader, belong to this class and are being gradually prodded into a dull rage, let us say no more on the subject but hasten up stairs at once. As has been remarked in another place, if we are in a real English house we may have to hunt about a bit to find these same stairs.

The problem on the second floor is briefly to get as many and as large rooms as possible, and all other considerations are secondary. There is no need of the clear height from floor to ceiling on the second floor being over eight feet six inches, and it may well be eight feet or even seven feet six inches, which will be a great aid to coziness and will lend to the rooms an appearance of size which they do not possess.

The owner's quarters will naturally be the best, and we shall expect to find him with the southern sun, a pleasant view, a fireplace and his own bathroom and dressing-room, a sitting-room perhaps, and one or two closets — a man and his wife should each have one. The other members of the family will probably not have individual bathrooms.

There should be one bathroom in any case opening into the main hall for the public, even if it is ordinarily private property. It is a good idea to arrange two rooms and a bath at one end of the house that can be shut off from the rest and used as a suite, where, in case of a contagious disease, the nurse may live with her patient in isolation. All the bedrooms should be plentifully supplied with closets having poles for coat-hangers, a wide shelf for ladies' hats and plenty of hooks. A linen-closet should lead out of the upper hall; either a big closet that one may walk into, with drawers and shelves, or, if we are pressed for room, merely a series of recessed, deep shelves from floor to ceiling, having paneled drop fronts flush with the wall surface. This will need no other door. Such an arrangement will hold all the linen that most families require. The shelves, instead of being solid, are often formed of slats so that fresh linen placed on them may have a further chance to air and dry.

A matter which is not ordinarily given sufficient care in the planning of a bedroom is the consideration of wall space for the accommodation of the necessary furniture. Radiators are almost as greedy of wall space as windows and doors, and are *always* bigger than we planned! Registers, too, have a way of turning up in unexpected places and taking to themselves the most desirable spot in the room. It is some satisfaction to know at least that the ancient architects did not get off free on this score, for Sir Henry Walton, writing in 1624, says, " Palladio observeth that the Ancients did warm their rooms with certain secrete Pipes that came through the walles (transporting heate as I conceive it) to sundry parts of the House, from one common Furnace — which whether it were a custom or a delicacie, was surely both for thrift and for use, far beyond the German stoves: and I should prefere it likewise before our own fashion, if the very sight of a fire did not adde to the Roome a kinde of Reputation." We all feel the " Reputation " of such a room and the call of the open fire. Our own Charles Dudley Warner had the same thing in mind when he deplored the cheerful blaze giving way to our modern methods, and pictures the future Yuletide season when *pater familias* on a blustering Christmas eve gathers his faithful wife and merry brood about the — register! The register and radiator are everywhere and it will be hard enough to hold these ubiquitous nuisances in check even when their presence is anticipated.

The problem of the servants' rooms is one that often causes much difficulty. In the medium-sized house it is usually necessary that they have their rooms on the third floor. The objection to this is the noise resulting from having them over one's head.

There seems to be some mysterious, exhilarating influence that affects those who inhabit the third story, that finds its outlet in their dashing their boots to the floor. It seems strange in this age of luxurious living and practical eugenics that one-legged servants are not bred, for on this score at least they would be certainly twice as desirable. Another drawback to the third-floor servants' room is the heat in summer; under the roof as they are, even with a partial air space between the ceiling and the roof, these rooms are bound to be hot, especially at night after the sun has been blazing on the roof all day.

A better arrangement, if we can afford the space, is to put the servants' rooms with the bath on the second floor over the service portion of the first floor, and reached by the back stairs, this group of rooms being connected with the rest of the second floor by a single door. This brings their working and sleeping quarters close together and gives them more freedom, while the master's portion of the house is unconscious of their existence. This arrangement is not a difficult one to bring about, but the problem is somewhat complicated if there is a single manservant to be housed. A room on the first floor in the kitchen wing is often the best solution here, but it is a point that should be carefully considered for any given case.

Methods of Construction

IN Chapter II we followed the methods of construction of the half-timber house in the fifteenth and sixteenth centuries, during its period of evolution and growth, at a time when the state of civilization was very different from what it is to-day — when the methods of building were more primitive and the choice of materials much more restricted to the immediate vicinity of the work in hand. It is true that bricks were imported from Holland at an early period, but these were for the palaces of the nobility or the important buildings belonging to church or state.

The idea that these limitations in the matter of tools or materials was a handicap to good work, from the artistic point of view, or that our greater facility in these matters gives us an advantage over the earlier builders, is not at all true. Good art is not dependent on good tools; as a matter of fact, is quite independent of them. The limitations of these early builders was in reality a source of strength, and a powerful aid, even if an unconscious one, to honesty and directness in their work. They did not know the temptations which beset the modern builder, any more than they knew the difficulties that hamper the modern designer. They were not confused and diverted from the end in view by the multiplicity and complexity of the means at their disposal. There was only one way, and not a hundred others that were " just as good," by which " no one could tell the difference." One honest thing, perfectly adapted to its own special use, was not tricked out into imitating some other honest thing which happened to be more expensive. If the work of the early builders was good, their path at least was not beset with so many temptations to dishonesty at every turn. To-day the false economy to be secured by the use of the clever substitute for the real thing is a pitfall it requires much strength of character to avoid. We are a little skeptical nowadays about the " gods seeing everywhere," or, rather, we do not care if they do, so long as our neighbor, Mr. Worldlywise, does not.

Although the time has not yet arrived in this country as in Europe, when it is as cheap to build of brick or other burnt clay products as to build of wood, it is not far distant. When this condition does exist it will be a great help to the general architecture of this country, and the appearance of flimsiness, inseparable from timber work, will give way to the substantial impression produced by the more solid and enduring materials.

The finical, emasculated appearance which is a characteristic of wood frame construction, is one to which our eyes have become so accustomed that it is only on returning from a trip to foreign countries that we are struck with the flimsy appearance of our frame houses. There is a beauty of wood and another beauty of brick and stone, but the latter are the most appropriate and sensible for the onerous use to which a building is put.

However, the time has not yet arrived in any locality when stone, or baked clay, covered with stucco or otherwise, can compete in first cost with wood — convincing advertising pamphlets from the makers of clay products notwithstanding.

So if we must, with a sigh, give up the idea of building our house of the more permanent materials, and turn to the wood frame, let us at least cover it with something that will give us a wall which at once produces a plane surface of pleasant texture and at the same time is not dependent on the paint brush for its very life; that fire does not touch, that vines may cling to without harm; and that is warm in winter and cool in summer. Stucco is such a material. It has the happy quality of satisfying the practical man who *can* live by bread alone, and yet to whom we thus give cake as well.

Now let us look at this method of building our walls. In our half-timber house, the walls between the timbers will show stucco,

The points of interest on the exterior of a house gain in effectiveness by
being neither numerous nor scattered

Here again the half-timbering is used sparingly to give it value as an accent and much or all of the rest of the house will be of the same material with, perhaps, some brick, stone or siding, as the case may be, to give variety of color and texture.

Stucco The term " stucco " is a loose one, but the composition when used for outside plastering, is of cement, lime and sand in varying proportions. The proper proportioning of these ingredients, especially of the lime and cement, is a subject of much controversy and hardly any two plasterers combine them in the same proportions. This seems to be matter that has always been in debate and even as long ago as the Middle Ages we find masons commonly mixing such things as ox blood, beer, dung, sugar and milk with their lime.

The accounts for the repairs of the steeple of Newark Church in 1571 contain an entry, " 6 strike of malt to make mortar to blend with ye lyme and temper the same, and 350 eggs to mix with it." During the building of the Duke of Devonshire's house at Chiswick, the interior of which was stucco, the surrounding district was impoverished for eggs and buttermilk to mix with the stucco.

It used to be a common practice in our southern states to mix molasses with the mortar. The object of most of these admixtures was to retard the set in order to secure more ease in manipulation. It is a curious thing that a scientific formula to give the best results has never been promulgated, or at least never adopted. It is a matter of the utmost importance, and strangely enough there seems to be absolutely no authoritative decision as to what constitutes the best mixture for the peculiarly trying purpose for which stucco is to be used. While it is not strange that in a matter where every plasterer claims to be an expert, there should be a wide divergence of opinion, it does seem curious that among the really expert men of established reputation who have done quantities of work, and have years of experience behind them, there should not be a common formula which the consensus of opinion would accept as the best. It is, of course, a matter in which such a formula can be arrived at only empirically; an opinion from the study or the laboratory can carry little weight until it has been given the test of actual experience under the conditions which it will be called upon to meet.

There also, unfortunately, seems to be a disposition on the part of the plasterers to treat the matter as a trade secret, and any statements that it is possible to wring from them carry such involved and lengthy qualifications and are so contradictory one with the other, that a collection and comparison of hard-won data reveals such surprising discrepancies that one wonders how any of the walls stand. To compare the results and discover what they have in common in a broad, general way, seems to be about all that one can do towards giving a formula for outside plaster.

Such an average of the best obtainable opinion, then, would seem to indicate that the first or " scratch " coat should not have over half cement nor less than fifteen per cent. that the second coat is usually a little " stiffer " — that is, that it may have more cement in proportion to the lime, and that the third coat or the " slap-dash " will vary as to the amount of the cement according to the color which is desired for the finish.

To introduce one of the many qualifications, we might say that there is a school of plasterers who say that in order to have the coats adhere perfectly the one to the other and form a compact, homogeneous mass, it is important that all coats should be of exactly the same mixture. In order to show, however, that we have an open mind in these matters, let us give the formula recommended by one of our largest manufacturers of expanded metal lath. " Mix the scratch coat," say they, " in the proportion of one part Portland cement, three and one-half parts sand, one-half part putty, made with hydrated lime. The second coat should be mixed in the proportion of one part Portland cement to three parts sand, and the finish coats one part Portland cement and two parts sand. Lime putty, not exceeding five per cent, is often used to advantage in the finish coat."

Another popular mixture calls for half and half Portland cement and lime, with four times their combined volume of sand.

Many men use two parts of lime to one of cement, while others vary the proportions in the different coats. The tendency of the honest plasterer, new to this kind of work, is to put in too much cement. He argues that in most other mason work the more Portland cement in the mortar used, the better job, which is generally true. The trouble with this reasoning is that when Portland cement mortar is applied in great sheets such as we have on the side of a house, it has not enough elasticity. The cement makes it too rigid and brittle, and the changes of temper-

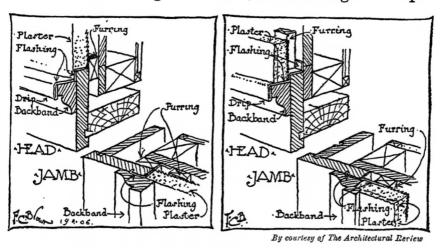

By courtesy of The Architectural Review

The most vulnerable points in a stucco wall are found at the intersection of stucco and the wood trim around windows and other openings. The protection of these points by flashing cannot be too carefully done

ature or slight shrinkages of the building cause it to crack or perhaps come away altogether. One is rather forced into the position, after seeing what a chaos of opinion prevails, revealing such a total lack of any real knowledge on the part of these workmen, of believing that it cannot after all make very much difference *what* his stucco is made of. Therefore it is a very cheering thing to be told that such is really the case! The mixture of the stucco, we are told, is really not so important after all, neither is the kind or make of the lath backing so essential; but the really necessary and important thing is that the plaster covering itself should at every point of contact with the woodwork, about the windows, water-table, cornice, posts and angles, be so absolutely impervious to the entrance of water that this arch foe of metal is repulsed at every point, keeping the metal upon which the plaster clings and owes its support sound from rust.

For this reason it is important that all horizontal timbers embedded in the plaster, whether or not they are flush with the plaster face, be carefully flashed with metal. This applies to water-tables, tops of window- and door-casing as well as to the half-timbering. The wider edge of such timbers must have a drip to drop the water clear of the wall, so as to prevent the water running down the face of the wall.

The vertical pieces must have rabbets run on their back edges so that the wet stucco may be forced into them and so stop any through crack that might appear should the wood, in time, shrink away from the immovable cement.

This stucco face can be put on over poured concrete which has had its face roughened either in the mold or afterwards, or put on a wall of cast concrete blocks which have had their faces corrugated so as to give a clinch for the stucco. Without some actual physical grip on the face to which stucco is applied, it will not stick. It has no adhesive properties of its own. It may be applied over a brick wall the joints of which have been raked out so that the stucco may be squeezed in, and the bricks in this case should be hard baked and even rough and twisted. It may be applied over terra cotta blocks which have been molded with a key on the face, or in fact over anything that will give the necessary grip for the mortar.

Much of our modern work is applied over a wall of wooden studs, and is ordinarily done in the following manner: The wall is framed with studs which are placed on the sill or girts and boarded on the outside exactly as for a shingled or clapboarded house. Over the boards on the outside is nailed one, or better, two thicknesses of some damp-proof building paper with all the joints between the sheets well lapped. Furring strips of wood, one inch square, are then nailed vertically nine inches on centres. Over this one-half inch wire mesh is stretched — better galvanized after it is woven — and securely fastened with galvanized staples to each strip.

We are now ready for the stucco. Some plasterers prefer the

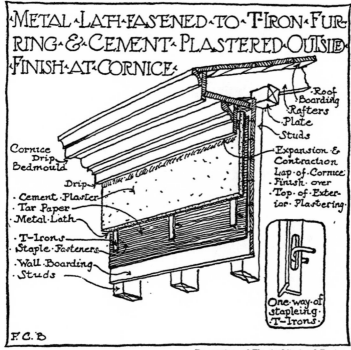

A detail of the wall and cornice where metal lath on T-irons was used upon the outside of the sheathing

furrings put on horizontally, as they say it enables them to stretch their wire up and down tighter, but it seems to the author that any settlement of the frame will be more likely to bring the horizontal strips to which the wire is fastened closer together, and thus cause a slight buckling, than is the case when the strips are vertical, and such shrinkage of the wall boards and settlement of the frame can not shorten the strips which run from top to bottom and are themselves the frame that really supports the stucco face.

Sometimes the manufacturers make a metal V- or T-shaped channel which is to be used instead of the wood furring, and this no doubt is good when properly applied. It is stapled in place through a slot in the metal which allows of slight movement up and down, should there be a settlement. The lath is wired to this metal. Instead of the wire mesh, expanded metal is often used, but it is not holding its own in popular favor. The danger of trouble with stucco applied over a metal lath instead of on brick or concrete is that the metal may rust away in time and the stucco

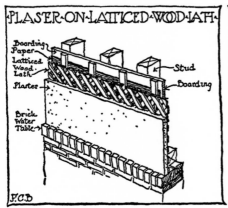

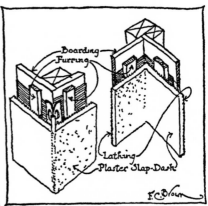

By courtesy of The Architectural Review

(a) There are those who claim that the use of diagonal wood lath is as good as, or perhaps better than, metal as a support for the stucco

(b) Extremely sharp corners are neither necessary nor desirable on stucco walls. There is a metal corner-bead that helps to preserve a true edge

fall off in great slabs. The users of the wire mesh claim that the first coat of mortar if properly applied squeezes through the mesh, falls over behind and thus completely embeds the wire and protects it from any dampness that through any inadvertence may have found its way back of the stucco. It is claimed that, while the expanded metal is stronger and stiffer, it is harder to effect this embedding process, and that rust makes little of its extra bulk and strength once it finds an opening for attack.

We might call the attention of the reader at this point to a fact which constitutes one of the very strongest claims of stucco and wood to the favorable consideration of the prospective house-builder. Whether the lathing be one sort or another, and whatever be the formula for the composition of our stucco, we obtain for our wall the very great advantage of two dead-air spaces in its thickness. These dead-air spaces constitute a most valuable insulation, not only against dampness but, what is of more importance, a very efficient protection against changes of temperature, which fact tends to produce a cooler house in hot weather and a warmer house in cold weather.

The first air space is that between the inside plaster on its wooden or metal lath fastened to the inside of the studs, and the boarding on the outside. This space of course we find in every frame house, no matter what the outside covering. The second space, peculiar to this method of work, is that between the outside boarding with its paper covering, and the back of the outside stucco which is held away one inch by the thickness of the furring strips. We thus get a double hollow wall.

Because of this possibility of rust in metal lath of any form there are those who stoutly maintain that exterior wooden lath on furrings is just as good if not better than metal, as it avoids this possibility of disaster.

There is another method that is often used and which has its staunch supporters, and is the cheapest for buildings that are not too large. This method consists in applying the metal lath directly to the studs — and when this is done an expanded metal of some little stiffness should be used and the studs be placed nearer together than in the first method and cross braced twice in a story's height. Nine inches on centre is about the right spacing for the ordinary two-story house. If the house is high and, in consequence, demands greater stiffness, we shall sadly miss the outside boarding with its added strength and protection against racking which it is bound to afford. Again, the necessity of placing the studs nearer together, nearly, if not quite, offsets the saving which has been effected by eliminating the boarding.

One of the strongest points in favor of this method is that

after we have plastered the outside of the lath we go inside and plaster directly on the back side of the same lath between each pair of studs. It will be seen that in this way we get the metal entirely embedded in the cement, at least theoretically. In practice, however, the inevitable shrinkage of the stud will in time open a small crack where the two come together, and although

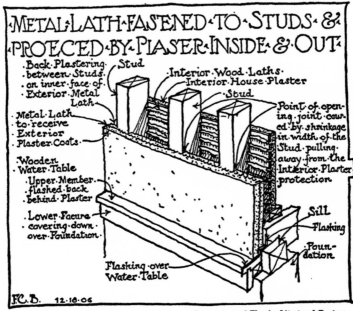

The method of fastening metal lath directly to the studs and then plastering on both sides of this support. There is a disadvantage in the loss of a dead-air space

this is of course on the inside, and has the whole thickness of the outside coat still between it and the weather, it is not quite fair to say that the metal is hermetically sealed. Any wet that may have got behind from some cause or other, such as the careless junction between a bit of outside finish and the stucco coat may still search it out. There can be no question, however, but that the protection is much more nearly perfect than in the other method. This inside back plastering must of course be done be-

"The Gables," Thelwall, England, one of the comparatively few modern houses where the timbering is solid and extending the full depth of the wall

Another view of "The Gables." Were it not that the timbering has been kept light in color the contrast of so much pattern would be far less satisfactory

One of the strongest features of the design is the straightforward, sturdy treatment of the chimneys

fore the inside lathing is nailed in place. By this method we also lose one of our precious dead-air spaces, which are really one of the very strongest utilitarian arguments in favor of covering our house with stucco. It should be said, before leaving this subject, that the danger of trouble with metal lath is not great, as the process is understood nowadays, and the stories of the failure of such work are of cases usually of some years back, before this work was as well understood as it is to-day. Even

Terra cotta blocks are beginning to compete seriously with wood construction and will no doubt soon be the less expensive form

now, however, it is not every plasterer that may be entrusted with this outside plastering, and we ought to be slow to take a man's own word for his competence without some more convincing proof of his ability.

But it is a question how much longer this method of applying stucco over a wooden frame will continue in vogue, as the difference in cost of building a house having the outside walls of wood covered with stucco, and of terra cotta covered with the same material, is becoming less every day. While lumber is showing a steady and natural tendency from year to year to advance in price, the burnt-clay products are gradually becoming not only cheaper but more widely distributed, better known, and much improved in every way.

A committee of the Boston Chamber of Commerce recently investigated the subject of the comparative cost of building, and their conclusions are of interest. A set of plans of a house which had already been erected was submitted to five different contractors and their estimates were then averaged for purposes of comparison. This average estimate for a frame building covered with clapboards was $6759.95. The average increase in cost for other methods was as follows:

	PER CENT.
Stucco on frame	2.92
Brick veneer on studding	5.83
Stucco on hollow blocks	6.34
Brick veneer on boarding	6.95
Ten-inch brick wall, hollow	9.16
Brick veneer on hollow block	10.77

While these increases were no doubt correct for the house under discussion we seldom in practice find these increases so slight as here given.

Of course there are other things for the builder who is chiefly interested in economy to consider besides the first cost. There is the matter of upkeep and of fire protection. Stucco on a wooden stud is the most fireproof material with which one can cover a frame house. The matter of repairs and upkeep is reduced to a minimum. There is no outside painting to be done except for the small amount of wood trim, and the wall itself requires absolutely no care, whether the stucco is applied over a wood frame or over some form of burnt clay.

So much for the backing of our stucco wall. Now as to the application of the stucco itself. The work should be put on in three coats, the first mixed with hair and troweled well into the lath or wall and " scratched." The second coat is troweled on after the first is dry, and the third or last coat troweled on, leaving it rough with the trowel marks showing here and there, not too ostentatiously. If the plasterer is told to leave the marks of his trowel he will, if his ideas of a good job will permit him to do it at all, laboriously and regularly let each sweep of the trowel be as distinct as it is possible, and even then these sweeps, which ordinarily have a certain pleasant freedom, will be cramped and timid because of his self-consciousness. If we wish it smooth from the trowel he will glory in making it a perfect mathematical plane, with all the corners sharp and true. A more popular and better way than either is to make the last coat what is known as "slapdash," or "pebble-dash." This is done by using a very thin mixture, of the consistency of heavy cream, with which has been mixed coarse sand containing small stones about the size that will pass through a one-eighth-inch mesh. This is taken out on a piece of board about the size of a shingle and thrown against the house with some force and left untouched. A broom of twigs is sometimes used instead of a paddle, this being dipped in the liquid which is then thrown on. The result is a very rough surface of marked and pleasant texture. This last coat may be colored before it is thrown on so that the pigment is part of the coating and gives a practically permanent color. A little yellow ochre gives a pleasant wall, if just enough is added to make an old-ivory color — enough to take off the coldness of pure white which the large amount of lime in the last coat will give if it is left untouched. There should not be enough to make it look yellow, unless for some reason this is desired. Pinks and grays and blues may also be had. These pigments must be earth or mineral coloring matter, and their free use is restricted only by the fact that when used in large quantities they tend to weaken the cement mixture, acting as inert matter, much as does clay or loam if it is allowed to get into the mortar bed. Vegetable colors are to be avoided, as the action of the lime seems to vitiate them and the sun still further fades and alters the original color. While the weakening effect on our stucco by the use of mineral coloring matter is so slight in the ordinary use of color as to be negligible, there are methods of getting color which do not detract even so much from the strength of the set. In the first place we may, instead of mixing our pigment into the body of the mortar, apply it to the surface of the last coat when it is still wet, as a surface coloring. This may be done by a blower of some sort or by being washed on with a brush. This is not a method that is much used, and the necessarily imperfect hold which the powder will have on the stucco, together with the difficulty of getting anything like an even distribution of pigment, and the consequent uneven and blotchy effect of the resulting wall, are inherent weaknesses in its use. A better way than this, if we should want a pink or brown or yellow wall, would be to mix in the proper amount of brick dust in the last coat to produce the desired shade of color. In the same way considerable effect can be obtained by using colored pebbles and sand in the finish coat. This will not affect the strength of our mixture, and there are, of course, many other materials of the same general character that are available in the same way and which will increase the range of colors at our disposal. It must be remembered that cement alone is of a cold gray color that does not form a good body color for our tints. They lose their clearness and individuality in the partnership, of which the pigment is too often the silent member. It is of course impossible for any but the practised plasterer to tell what color will result from any given proportion of admixture, and it is absolutely necessary that samples of considerable size be prepared and applied to some wall in the same manner and showing the same surface texture as it is proposed to finish the wall under treatment. Again, this must be looked at only after it has had plenty of time to set and dry; then only can the final color be seen. This should be considered in sun and shadow, wet and dry, and while the pigment will not itself probably fade or change, the natural darkening which will result from the rough walls collecting dust and dirt as time goes on, must also be taken into account. Pure white, light yellows, or soft pinks may be best obtained if there is a goodly proportion of lime in the last coat; that is, if it largely predominates over the cement. Lime is naturally an almost pure white, and an excellent foundation for the production of clear,

A true half-timber house in process of construction

The use of solid timbers extending through the walls is, here in America, almost out of the question because of the cost both of the timbers and the labor required

"Stonecroft," Appleton, Cheshire — an excellent example of vigorous half-timber work of to-day

unaggressive tints, free from the sodden, muddy look of which it is so hard to get rid when cement alone or in large proportions is present.

If it is argued that adding too much lime will not give the hardness or the toughness that is desired, and that only Portland cement will give, we may then use white cement which is a comparatively new brand, having the same strength as the ordinary Portland cement, and of a pure dazzling whiteness. The only drawback to its more extensive use at present is the cost, which is several times that of the old Portland cement.

It has not been thought necessary to warn the builder against Rosendale cement, as its use is now practically abandoned everywhere, and the cheapness, availability and infinite superiority of Portland cement for every purpose where a cement is used has driven it from the market.

For our half-timber work there are several methods which are common. In England to-day it is quite usual to pursue much the same methods that the joiners of the old days followed. The big honest timbers, often hand-hewn on the very land of the owners of the future house, are doweled and pinned in place with oak pins and the "daub," a little more scientifically mixed, no doubt, is filled in between. Many of the building laws of the local governing boards, however, demand nine inches of brick wall as a backing to these timbers. In this country, where our climate is more severe than in England, we must take additional precautions against the weather and not fail to carry at least some portion of our wall back of the half-timbers, thus obviating any chance of joints opening and acting as a channel to the enemy water. The illustration facing page 76 shows a house of this sort in the process of construction. Facing page 50 is a photograph of a house built by Mr. Harrison-Townsend, who says that the half-timbers used here were old railroad sleepers taken and used just as they lay. One may imagine the beautiful color and texture, and the impression of primitive strength that is always so satisfying. The longer horizontal timbers were pieces of old staging, equally rough, and stained with those particularly fast colors of which nature alone knows the secret. In the same way Englishmen are fond of using old roof tile and slate which they buy from the owners of old cottage roofs, usually by offering to replace these roofs with brand-new ones, much as we have heard of furniture collectors in this country exchanging a new varnished chair for old Chippendales in the rural districts. This use of old material for the sake of its atmosphere, for work of our character, is one of the great lessons that the present-day English architects have to teach us. But after the architect has learned the lesson he will still have the task of educating the client. It is strange that nothing is easier than to find people who would admire houses of this sort immensely, but yet who would hesitate and gasp if told that part of the price of such charm and simplicity is the using of battered, second-hand lumber. " But what would the neighbors? " etc. The English understand the indescribable charm that hangs like a perfume about old things, even if they are but fragments of old things, like our battered timbers. The richness that goes with mild decay speaks to the sensitive man as the new, characterless stuff without experiences or memories of its own can never do. The owner does not like to pay just as much for old, battered, second-hand stuff as for the new, clean, straight stock, and yet such charming houses as that facing page 30 owe their elusive charm to the texture and color which belong to the old tile, unplaned siding, and rough sticks. We pay enormous prices for antiques to put into our houses. Why should we not build them in and make of them the warp and woof of our home? Whatever be the reason of their appeal, we may safely leave the explanation to the professors of esthetics; the fact is enough for us that the subtle charm and beauty of such houses, built in this way, is undeniable and is felt by the most careless observer. If we are wise we will see if there is not something here that we may learn to our profit even if the esoteric psychological reasons are hidden from our understanding and we work empirically in the true artistic fashion.

The usual criticism of the use of modern half-timber work, namely that it is impossible to build new houses with the charm which we admire so much in old ones, because such charm is primarily due to their age with its incident effects, is not a just one.

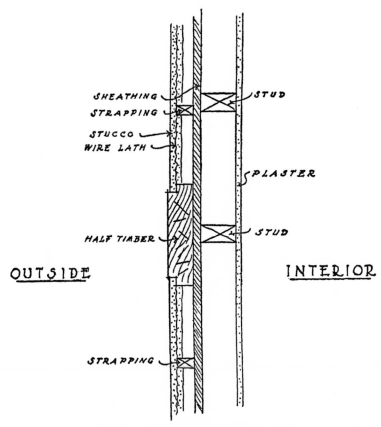

A very common substitute for whole-timber construction is the use of a rabbeted plank planted upon the outside of the sheathing

It is true that we cannot reproduce, nor would we wish to try, the pleasant air of general dilapidation so much more delightful to look at than to live with. We may, however, obtain the general sense of beauty, picturesqueness, and, above all, of the Anglo-Saxon home feeling which by unconscious atavism so fills the

Half-timber work is seen at its best where the strong black-and-white contrasts are limited to a few points of accent

heart of the exiled descendants of English blood in the presence of these wonderful cottages. It is the " Home sweet home " that we have never seen, but our hearts are the touchstone that prompt our slower brains. Such houses as those shown facing pages 73 and 77 are all new, all perfectly tight, warm and practical. They may have vacuum cleaners and wireless telephones for aught we know, but they have not lost the charm that so often slips through the fingers of the most up-to-date builder or painstaking writer of specifications.

There is another method of building our half-timber walls that is less satisfactory from the esthetic point of view, but which is nevertheless a good substitute as far as appearance and practical service is concerned. This is the use, when we are dealing with a frame house, of a rabbeted plank planted on the furring thus forming our " half-timber." The plaster filling is between, applied on the metal lath, the rabbet on the back of the stick helping to secure tightness. These planks are sometimes secured in place after the first coat of plaster is on, the other two coats filling up the space flush or nearly flush with the face of the planks. This is the common method in vogue and while not comparable to the use of real sticks of timber with the attendant knots and checks, may be made an acceptable substitute if we take care to avoid hard edges and corners, and either have the faces hand-hewn with the adze, or use the planks " mill-faced," that is, with the rough, furry marks of the circular saw still in evidence and not touched by a plane or smoothed in any way. And, above everything else, they must not be touched with lead and oil paint. The wood should either be treated with some of the patent liquid wood preservatives on the market, or given two coats of raw linseed oil, which will serve as an excellent preservative against rot if brushed over about as often as one would paint outside woodwork. To work in such a rough, masculine way as we have done up to this point, and then to cover our honest wood with such a smug, artificial thing as a coat of paint would be a great error in common sense and taste. The key which we strike at the outset must set the pitch for the entire work, and consistency is as valuable a jewel here as elsewhere.

In laying out the design of these half-timbered walls it is always well to remember that we are handling a very vigorous and aggressive form of decoration, whatever else it may be. It should be labeled, "Dangerous — Handle with care." It is sure to arrogate to itself the lion's share of attention, and so must be used carefully and with due restraint. It is valuable and should be handled as if it were a jewel — as a precious thing. It should be used to produce an accent, a high light in the picture. This aspect of half-timbered walls has never seemed to be duly appreciated in modern work. The timbering is often seen spread evenly over the four walls of a house from top to bottom, so that its chief value and charm, its contrast with less exciting wall surfaces, is entirely lost. To accent one word in a sentence gives force, to accent all gives none.

In pictorial art this point is well exemplified in the sketches of the greatest of all modern pen-and-ink artists, the Spaniard Vierge. Their life and sparkle are largely due to the one or two small patches of solid black which he is careful to introduce somewhere among his middle tones. They give an accent, a snap to the whole where their more generous use would produce a result at once flat and commonplace.

The modern houses shown facing pages 21 and 59 are examples of the sparing use of half-timber. In the first it is used to glorify the front entrance of the house, in the second as a point of interest against the foil afforded by the plain walls about it.

It was common in roofing the dormers and gables to project the roof over the walls a foot or so in order to protect the walls below from the weather. The projection was greater in the earlier work, and receded for some reason or other as time went on, until we find the barge-board which formed the outer finish of the overhang flat against the wall. In the best work much care and ingenuity were expended in the decoration of these barge-boards, or verge-boards, as they are sometimes called. Many beautiful

The timbering is too often seen spread evenly over the four walls of a house from top to bottom, so that its contrast with simple wall surfaces is lost

It is a relevation to those of us who are accustomed to machine work on every hand to see
the enrichment of detail on even the simplest English cottage of an earlier age

examples still remain of the piercing in trefoil cusps, which are carved and played with by the ingenious carpenters, who treated them in much the same way that old Izaak Walton tells us to treat the frog with which we are baiting our hook, when he says, " Handle him as if you loved him." The finial against which the barge-boards abut at the top is also a favorite object of the carver's attention.

Siding, much like our own clapboards, is much used in England on wall gables to obtain a variety of effect. The best wood for this is elm, for though it twists and warps, this does no harm, as we are relying on it only to throw off the rain and not to keep out the cold. It is sawn rough and the natural edge sometimes left untouched, and, with nothing more done to it than to add a coat of oil, will take on a soft silvery hue, most harmonious with the other material and the surrounding foliage.

Exterior Details

THERE will probably never again be a roof covering for a small house quite as beautiful as thatch. We say "again" because thatch is doomed. Its utilitarian objections are too many.

Thatch Its dampness and consequent rotting make it unsanitary. It is always invested with vermin; it is apt to leak after a prolonged spell of dry weather; and the danger of fire is very great and ever present.

In England its use has been legislated against, so that where building laws are operative it is forbidden. Thatching is becoming a lost art, and in this country it is rarely that a man can be found who understands how to do it. What little has been done here has been of a small and playful character, as garden houses, children's play-houses and the like. With a sigh, then, we will pass on to more practical methods of keeping out the rain.

In England they are fortunate in being able to get hand-made tile. These are infinitely preferable to the tile we get in this country with their even color and hard, flat, *Tile and* machine-made look. Old tile are also often used. *Shingles* If the use of old tile needs any apology we have it in their superiority from the point of view of the practical man. Their age has somehow or other made them weather-tight and they are soft and porous enough for lichen to cover them, that silvery fungus to which, Ruskin beautifully said, " slow fingered, constant hearted, is entrusted the weaving of the dark eternal tapestries of the hills." To coax lichen to our new tile will mean that we must make them so soft and porous that they will not for a long time be damp-proof; to make them hard enough to resist the weather will be to condemn them to carry their glittering surfaces fresh and raw to the end. Then, hand-made tile have a slight concave curve in their width which is of great aid in throwing off the water. Machine tile, for ease in packing and transportation, are made as flat as a board. The dry, thin, desiccated-looking tile roofs which we see all about us have about as much real charm and character as the machines that make them. However, we are getting past this stage and better tile are now coming on the market. Whether it is that the machines are being perfected and have added the supreme "art that conceals art," or whether the clumsy inaccurate hand of man is allowed to play some part in their creation, we do not know; but the fact that we will no longer have to import roof tile from England is encouraging. As in other matters of this sort it is necessary only to create a sufficiently urgent demand and make it sufficiently felt, to have it supplied. This means that the desire of a few, no matter how intense, will not avail, but that there must be a widespread and insistent call all along the line.

If for reasons of immediate, if shortsighted, economy we feel we must fall back upon the stock wooden shingle, its lifelessness and excessive neatness may be somewhat mitigated by laying the shingles so that the butts do not follow an exact line but fall hit or miss, a half-inch more or less above and below. This does not mean that first one shingle is to be laid half an inch above the line and the next half an inch below, and so on *ad nauseam*, but that there should be *no* method. Let the carpenter rule his line for the butts and then slap the shingle on the roof and drive in his nails as he would if he were in a tremendous hurry. To convey this point of view to the workman and get this done as we wish will be an extremely difficult and tiresome task. It will require no end of explaining and reasoning with the carpenter before he can be got to humor us to the extent of doing this properly, as his ideas of a good job will be thoroughly outraged. It really would save time and attain the same result to make him slightly drunk and set him to work. Another way is to have the stone mason do the shingling. Another method of getting some variety into our roofs with common shingles is to lay them, butts to a line, but varying without any system, the widths of the courses.

Still better, and hardly more expensive than the ordinary shingles, is the hand-split cypress shingle of the South. It is very thick and large, being about two feet six inches long and of generous and varying widths. The extra size, with the resulting increase of area exposed to the weather, means fewer shingles to cover any given surface, and it is this greater covering capacity that helps to bring down the cost. The gain is that of the pleasant texture which is obtained from the split or hand-shaved surface, the heavy butts, and the sense of scale that is imparted by the greater size of the shingles and their spacing. While they are effective on the roof, they are even more so on the walls of a house. As yet they are little used in the North and West, but are destined to become more popular as the present shingles of commerce become of poorer and poorer quality as the years go by.

The use of slate is destined to become daily more popular. The wooden shingle is not only becoming more expensive with the increasing scarcity of lumber, but its quality is *Slate* steadily deteriorating. The danger of fire from a wooden roof covering also strengthens the demand for something more substantial. Slate shares with tile this immunity from fire, and has the advantage over it of being less expensive. The cost per square (one hundred square feet) of shingle, slate and flat tile, on the roof, is about $10, $15 and $30, allowing some variation for quality and locality. Red slate is also more expensive than the other colors.

Slate, like tile, should be laid on the roof boarding over some waterproof paper or felting, asphalt or the like. Many of the patented preparations are good. The slate are then nailed with copper nails through the waterproofing into the roof boards and set in slaters' cement around angles or curves.

Oswald C. Hering, Architect

A modern country home near Philadelphia, where a fairly heavy flat red tile has been used for the roof covering

An excellent example of the use of graduated slates — large, thick ones near the eaves, with the courses becoming narrower and thinner towards the ridge

The nails should never be of iron or steel even when galvanized, and must not rust out, as the fastening should be as indestructible as the slate.

The old thin blue slates of the middle of the last century have given place to a thicker, rougher slate which is to be had in variegated and pleasant colors and is superior in every way. Shades of red, green, purple, blue and gray are on the market, and we may make our roofs of one solid color or mix two adjacent tints to give a pleasant life and variety to the surface. It is well to make sure that our slate is unfading in color, as this is not always the case.

The greatest gain of the slate of to-day over the old ones is in their increased size, thickness and surface texture. This has done away with the thin, hard-looking roofs of our earlier time. A favorite method of laying is to graduate the sizes of the slate from eaves to ridge, that is, to lay the largest, thickest slate in wide courses at the eaves and allow them to decrease in size as they approach the ridge. If we seek the effect of variety and ruggedness, it is important to use large slate but is even more important that they be *thick*. An inch at the butt is not too much on cottage work, and the effect is worth what it costs. Facing this page is a roof of this sort.

The ridge may be finished with a copper or lead roll, which had best be left unbroken and without ornament.

There is no more satisfactory roof for any house than one done in this way, combining, as it does, all the virtues of beauty, fitness and utility.

Stamped tin imitations need hardly be taken seriously as they are neither handsome, honest, economical nor efficient.

The asbestos shingle has done well but has hardly been on the market long enough to have been thoroughly tried out. It suffers from its even lifelessness of color, and looks like a painted surface. It is fireproof and its makers claim long life for it.

We have already touched on the value in the design of the outside chimney stack, and of what a typical feature such a chimney was in the old half-timber houses. The variety of shape and design of these chimneys is almost infinite, from the very elaborate and complex stacks as shown facing page

Chimneys   89, in which the brick are especially molded or ground to fit their places in the design, to those in houses like that facing page 72, where the bricks are alike and all of the common variety. The intricacy of the design is made entirely by placing the brick in different relative positions, sometimes chipping off a hidden part to keep the bond about the flues and insure stability.

Such elaborate stacks as those shown facing page 89 are rendered more difficult to-day by the use of terra cotta flue linings, which make any curving or twisting of the flue almost impossible without somewhere constricting the sectional area and thus hurting the draft. It may best be done by using a circular flue lining.

We have a tendency in this country to be a little timid with our outside stacks; they too often look as if the builders were ashamed of them instead of being proud of them, glorifying and honoring them. They are capable of being the most effective motive in the design if they are made ample in size and plenty of thought is given to their design. There are not many parts of a house that are so tractable and so flexible as an outside chimney; we may do with it almost what we will, expand or contract, raise or lower, shape it to suit any caprice and enrich it as much or as little as we please. It can easily be made to give scale to the whole. The idea that an outside chimney is apt to have a poor draft need not trouble us, for with modern flue linings and eight inches of brick or more around them we can avoid any danger of such trouble.

These chimneys are most successful when a common waterstruck brick is used and the entire " run of the kiln " is utilized. That is, the bricks must not be culled but *all* the bricks used as they come from the baking; light, dark, and even twisted. The more variety of color and surface the better, not forgetting the black headers which have been nearest the fire. Lay these up as

The chimney may be one of the chief elements in the design of the exterior.
"The Gables," Thelwall, England

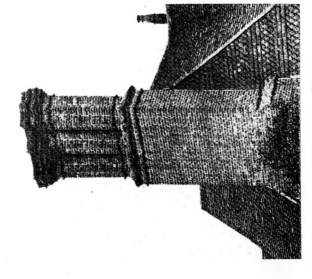

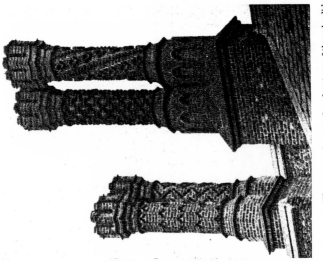

We are very slow to take advantage of the splendid opportunities for variety and embellishment in our chimneys.
In no other architectural style are the chimneys made so much of in the design

they come to hand, again avoiding the conscious selection of every header a black one, or any other rule. It is interesting to see what splendid lively brickwork is done when the masons think it will not show, behind furring and the like. If the surface is a large one, without breaks or angles, the need of a little variety in the surface will be felt. In this case we may make a criss-cross pattern, either using black headers or by projecting them slightly from the face of the wall, so that the slight shadow will make a simple pattern. Again, we may lay courses of brick on end or on edge, or project a row of the corners of brick laid at forty-five degrees with the surface, or sink panels, or make designs, or project belt courses. There is considerable choice between narrow limits.

Then if we choose we may invest the surface with the desired interest by changing the color of the brick joints or by raking out certain of them. In fact it will not be hard in innumerable ways to add just as little or as much interest to our brick wall as we choose.

One of the things to avoid and that will render useless all the trouble we have taken, is the use of a pressed or fancy brick of any description. Another is the use of a red mortar that matches the bricks. Again, it is a temptation to say that only red bricks will do, because it is so nearly a complete fact. Lately, however, bricks of a purple tinge, with excellent surfaces, have come on the market and one can imagine they would look very well under certain conditions; but as for gray, yellow, white or mottled brick — they will never do. Nothing is so safe and satisfactory as red, the individual bricks of which may vary from salmon pink to dark plum. Lay these with an honest white mortar, half-inch-wide flush joint, and the effect will be of a soft pink wall of great life and interest.

If chimney-pots are used, they should be of the plainest possible design and without any patent arrangement at the top supposed to help the draft. If our flue is as big as it ought to be its draft will not need any such assistance.

The chimney-pots themselves must have a sectional area as large as that of the flues they cover, and the contraction at the top should be very slight. It may be that such contraction at the top of a flue helps the draft, as is said, but only a very little should be permitted. The struggle we are sure to have had to get our flue big enough will have gone for naught, if it is to be choked at the top.

Chimney-pots are only of assistance for the draft when the chimney is lower than some neighboring roof ridge or other projection. The wind blowing over such an obstruction sometimes forces an eddy of air down the flue. If we raise the outlet high enough we avoid the trouble. It is in thus prolonging the flue that the chimney-pot has its real use.

The windows in the old work were filled with casement sash. From a comparatively early time this sash was of metal, and has *Windows* so continued — the section of the bar being improved upon of late years as well as a more complicated frame to receive it, with the ever-present idea of excluding wind and rain. These sash opened out in nearly every case and were fastened with an ornamented lever working on the cam principle.

The detachable butt was an invention inspired by necessity or, at least, convenience. For in the reign of the first Tudors glazed window sash were a luxury, and your nobleman, when he traveled from one of his country seats to another, not only carried his bed and other furniture, but, with his tapestries to keep out the drafts, he unhinged his windows and brought those along! In the early times horn was used in the windows in lieu of glass. In manuscripts of the time of Henry VIII we find such items as "a thousand lantern horns for the windows of timber houses," and "gilding the lead on lattice work of the horn windows." These casements were divided by lead muntins (bars dividing the panes in a sash) in the earliest work, when they were of diamond pattern, but later the divisions became rectangles, usually higher than they are broad. This is a more quiet shape and less tiresome

Casement windows and small panes both belong inseparably to the
half-timber house

It is not difficult to imagine how thoroughly incongruous and hideous large sheets of plate glass would look in a building of this kind to the eyes which must look through them; for as these muntins and the shapes they assume are very plainly stamped on the eyes of the outlooker, the black lines against the light, this is a matter of importance and will be felt by the least sensitive in such matters. The lead divisions later became extraordinarily complex, and great ingenuity was displayed in their design.

Owing to the difficulty and in fact impossibility which was experienced in making sheets of glass of any size, these panes were small, and necessity in this case proved a friend, for, esthetically at least, the clever maker of great sheets of perfect glass has been of no assistance to the artist or architect. Except in a shop window or a Pullman car, large sheets of plate glass are unsatisfactory. They destroy in the house all sense of seclusion, coziness or warmth, ruining the scale and making a summer-house or observatory out of one's quiet study. The letting in of all outdoors dwarfs and makes poor our interiors. One is never quite sure whether he is indoors or out; he is really astride the window sill and has an uneasy feeling that the whole world is looking in at him. For it is a poor window that does not work both ways. The modern idea, born of the fresh-air crusade — that houses cannot have too much light, not *sun* but *light* — is one of which many amateur house-builders learn the folly and unwisdom after their experiment in these directions is completed and it is too late. Like the sculptor, the architect must strike right the first time, for after the work is finished he will have learned his lesson, but the time will have passed for applying it. Too much light in a house is esthetically bad; it makes one's furniture and belongings look meagre and dingy — as witness our neighbor's goods and chattels. on the sidewalk on moving day. One would not have believed how tawdry his best parlor set really is, and as for the family portraits he has been so proud of — mere anæmic daubs! No. Colors and textiles as we have them in household hangings, rugs and stuffs generally, furniture and woodwork with its carving and enrichment, seem dreary and feeble by too abundant daylight. The ballroom is another place and a very tawdry one the next morning when the candles are out and the sun looks in. I have no doubt this over lighting of our rooms could be shown to be equally bad for the eyes, with its accompanying reflections and high-lights. A room is not comparable with its cross lights to outdoors, and the same amount of light is much more distressing to the eye.

In placing our windows we shall obtain more of an effect of privacy and warmth if we keep the stool or sill two feet or more above the floor. If it is over three feet we shall have difficulty in seeing out when we are seated, which is a source of annoyance. In the bedrooms this height may be raised without its being unpleasant and is accompanied by an increased sense of privacy. Of course the higher a window is in the wall the more light it contributes to the room. There is also a gain in ventilation with windows that can be opened near the ceiling.

On the exterior the levels of the heads of the windows should not change if possible for each story, unless it is to mark a staircase within or some reason of that sort; otherwise it will give the building a chaotic, restless, jumpy look that is the one unpardonable sin in the houses we have under consideration.

Our smaller panes, as seen from the outside, give a sense of scale, and by keeping the panes of glass as nearly as possible the same size and shape all over the building, whatever the size of the windows may be, the eye is insensibly given something to use as a basis of comparison by which to judge of relative sizes of other parts of the work.

A common criticism, that seems to obtain in the lay mind against casement sash, is that they are not tight against the weather. There is no doubt some truth in this criticism against such sash, when they are made to swing in; but when they swing out — as they always should do — it is not at all a difficult matter to make them as tight as a double-hung window — that is, one that is divided into two sash which slide up and down in grooves and are balanced by weights. In England it is customary, even in inexpensive work, to make the casement sash of metal and the frame to receive them also of metal, each cunningly rabbeted so that they come together in such a way as to keep out wind and rain equally on top, sides and bottom. A more serious charge is that it is hard to keep them open in a high wind, at least with the usual adjuster.

The use of the metal frame is less common in this country, but the wooden sash and frames which we use may be equally effi-

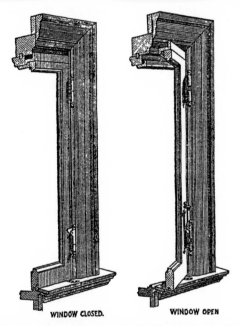

WINDOW CLOSED.   WINDOW OPEN

Ordinarily the casement windows had better open out unless there is some particular reason for having them open in. The whole sash may be raised on its hinges to slip out of the groove on the sill

cacious against the weather. The gain to be had by using casements is that the whole opening of the window may be utilized for ventilation, whereas in the sash window, only half can be opened at a time. We may more readily use them in groups, and when so used they are much more easily handled and the desired appearance obtained with greater ease and much less apparent straining after effect. They are smaller and less heavy and clumsy to manage, and the amount of wall space which we propose to devote to windows can be much more accurately and gracefully secured by using this form of opening.

Just what the psychological reason is for the charm and picturesqueness which seem to be inseparable from these casement windows, with the light sparkling on their small panes, or swung open to give a black hole into the room behind, with its mysterious lure of the unknown, we do not know. The scientific reason why they please us, does not interest us here. The fact for us is that they do possess a magic all their own, and that we freely and eagerly accredit them with being harbingers of delights within.

Bay-windows are always charming and are capable of an almost infinite variety in shape, size and method of treatment and design. No two are alike. They more often than not take the form of oriel windows corbeled out from the wall in our half-timber work, and their brackets in the old days gave a chance for the droll fancy of the carvers to express itself, and many quaint conceits are the result. These bays may be either continued to the floor or may stop above it to give a window-seat — a delightful arrangement — or they may be cut off just below the window so that only a wide stool or flower-shelf is left.

Dormer windows are usually a practical necessity if we are to make much use of our attics. They have always been used, but it may be taken as a general rule that most roofs gain in dignity and repose by their absence. They are usually treated so as to attract as little attention as may be. Their small walls are often shingled so that they will melt into the surrounding roof even when the walls below are of some other material. In the design of the houses of which we are writing, we shall do everything possible to produce the long low effect in contra-distinction to the high narrow one. We place the house as low in the ground as possible, with only one step to the front door; accent our horizontal lines by producing horizontal shadows, with overhangs and eaves, and deprecate anything as interesting even as a dormer window to attract the eye so high.

The doors in these old houses were usually made of solid planks

To the Englishman the doorway has always been a very important architectural feature
of his home and he spared no pains in enriching it with carved detail

A new doorway and an old one. It is in this typical shelter form that we may secure one of the most characteristic features of the best English tradition

without panels — that is, solid wood from side to side and often studded with nails. Three feet or so of solid wood means

Doors

shrinkage and expansion, and it is often hard, we find, nowadays at least, with an indifferently seasoned wood, to make our doors in this way and have them continue tight and well fitting. There is a great tendency to warp and twist. In the old days they apparently were not so nice in their requirements, and were thinking more of strength and less of draughts. The more pretentious doors were paneled and carved, often with narrower stiles and rails than our manufacturers of stock hardware will permit us to use — so hampered is the practical architectural designer. Strap hinges were used in the simple work, and of course in the more elaborate work the doors were hung with hinges which were very beautiful examples of the blacksmith's craft.

The Englishman has always felt the symbolism of the door to his home. He placed over it his coat of arms with mantlings. It was thus he announced himself, and beneath it in his porch he loved to give warm welcome to his friends and to press the stirrup cup on the parting guest. The doorway was the setting of many happy comings and sad partings. It held a very important place in the family shrine of home, and nothing could be more natural than that pains should not be spared for its adornment. It was usually covered by a porch to protect from the weather those who sought admittance.

The functions of a front door and its relation to the rest of the house have changed not at all with the passing centuries, and it is as worthy to command our best to-day as it ever was. The porch lends itself with much grace and distinction to architectural treatment, and we give a number of examples of timbered porches, some old, some new. The old lych gates to the churchyard entrances are among the best examples of these timbered hoods and shelters.

Whether or not a terrace belongs with "exterior details," may be open to question — at least as to its being a detail. It certainly is not if Webster is right in defining "detail" as "a minute portion." But if we have this definition at hand we may put it to some use by letting it stand for exactly what *Terrace* a terrace should not be. It is usually made too small and can never be made too large.

We have already, in speaking of dining-rooms, had something to say about the pleasures of dining out-of-doors and of the value of some sort of covering, screening or glazing in many localities. If the terrace has a duty to the dining-room, it must not neglect the living-rooms or hall, and should form an addition to one or all of these rooms. Nor will it have fulfilled its true function or exhausted its full possibilities for usefulness unless it can combine the greatest possible amount of privacy with the best that the house affords in the way of view. It will in any case serve as the vestibule of the garden, which in turn will act as an intermediary between the house and the country beyond. The garden should take each by the hand and bring them together. It is a great temptation, now we are almost in the garden, to say something about this great outdoor living-room, with its decorations of nodding hollyhock, foxglove, bursting snapdragon, dancing primrose and the thousand and one other blossoms, not forgetting the great rose family with their stately flowers and aristocratic names — these names which are so transformed by the Saxon tongues of the English cottagers. Thus the gallant crimson *Giant de Batailles* becomes "Gent of Battles." *Gloire de Dijon* changes to "Glory to thee, John," and a rose named from the great rosarian, Dean Reynolds Hole, is called "Reynard's Hole," while the beautiful *General Jacqueminot* becomes "General Jack-me-not." However, an Englishman has told us that a rose by any other name would smell as sweet, so we will not quarrel about the labels.

Further than to say that the garden should be thought of as an outdoor room, that it should have as intimate a connection with the house as is possible, and that the house should turn its friendliest face in its direction, we must not go. Volumes and volumes are written, and very properly, about gardens alone, and when we remember that of late years they have even acquired a self-anointed high-priest called a Landscape Architect who has constituted himself keeper of the *sacro sanct* mysteries of garden craft, let the author then, a mere architect, flee for his life up the path and safe onto the terrace before he stops for breath!

The terrace floor may be of brick, laid in cement mortar over a bed of broken rock and sand. The brick may be laid in herring-bone or basket pattern, or varied to suit the particular case, and when so used are best laid flat, as the resulting floor is smoother. Again, for cheaper and less formal work, the brick may be laid on a bed of sand and the joints between merely flushed full of sand or loam from which in time will spring up moss and small vegetation. This floor will have to be held in place by a border of cut stone, brick laid in cement or something having sufficient rigidity to hold in the loose brick. Such a floor, while it will in time settle in places and be less true than the other, can be more easily mended, it being a simple matter to lift a few bricks when they have settled and insert the necessary amount of filling to bring them to a level with the rest. Heavy frost will not be as apt to make trouble with a flexible floor of this sort as with the more rigid one of cemented joints.

Tile also make an admirable terrace floor, being smoother than brick, and may be had of a splendid red color. One must be sure his tile are baked sufficiently hard to withstand frost and hard knocks, and should be from six to twelve inches square and of an inch or more in thickness. Tiles imported from Wales have long been favorites, but lately a very satisfactory domestic tile has appeared, tougher in fact than the foreign one, but of not quite so good a color or texture. Tile keep their original color better than brick in actual practice, the latter holding more of the grime and dirt.

Another excellent surface for our terrace is flagstone. Any evenly stratified stone split off in random sizes and shapes will do. Bluestone or any firm shale is commonly used. This may be laid either in mortar on a prepared foundation, like brick; or better, laid all shapes and sizes, dovetailed together as nearly as possible, the joints being allowed to take care of themselves, which means that grass and vegetation will quickly fill in the interstices, producing a very pleasing and practical flooring for outdoors. Black and white squares of marble, while handsome enough in Italian or very formal work, are a little too grand to be in the same key with the rest of the house. Terraces of wood are desirable only when one cannot afford anything else. They are, when laid tight and uncovered, subject to rapid decay. Laid with open joints, their life will be prolonged, but they will be drafty and unsightly.

We are surely at the very edge of our province when we come to the terrace posts and rails, but we will keep one foot at least on the terrace and so save our consciences from the sin of poaching. Such posts may be built up either of brick with stone or cast cement cap, or made of cut stone or of cast cement — never of cobbles or field stone. With our type of house such a thing would be a triumph of vulgarity. Our rail, if it is not a wall of some kind, may be of stone with balusters of either brick or of turned stone, taking care that it is of the proper height and width to sit upon. If economy is necessary wood rails and turned balusters will answer very well. Chestnut or locust will stand the longest. We may have no rail of any sort if there is little or no change of level between the ground and the floor of our terrace.

Rain-water heads and down pipes or conductors are just as necessary to-day as they ever were, but for some reason or other they have ceased to play the part they formerly did. *Rain-water* While they were formerly given a place of honor *Heads* and were a source of pride, they now seem to be admitted grudgingly and apologetically. Where formerly they were big, splendid, important parts of the design, enriched and made much of, they are now merely timid, emasculated pipes, tucked away out of sight as nearly as may be. This is a great mistake.

In the half-timber house of to-day we shall make much more of our terrace, giving
it the best combination of privacy and view, with a paving
of tile, flagstone or brick

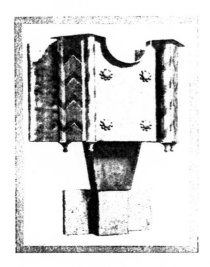

Another typical feature of the half-timber house that we have too long neglected
is the rain-water head of lead or its modern copper substitute

Their vertical lines, which may usually allow of considerable latitude in their placing, are of the greatest help to the designer, and the big heads give a splendid chance in the small house to obtain a sense of scale of which the architect should not be slow to take advantage.

While the lead heads, which to-day are as common in England as they formerly were, are hard to obtain in this country, we may make very satisfactory heads and pipes of copper, although it can never be as tractable for this purpose as the more ductile lead. Galvanized iron, which was a few years ago much used for this purpose, is to-day of such a poor quality that it will not last over six to eight years when used for this purpose. Zinc is not feasible largely for the same reason.

Interior Details

WHILE the exterior arrangement and design are little subject to rule, the interior effect is even less so. The difficulty of successful interior treatment lies in the minds of many householders, more in ignorance of what they should try to do than in any lack of interest in the result. The enthusiasm is not lacking, but it is too often without proper guidance.

The longing for a pretty and attractive home is strong in every housewife. She has a very clear mental picture, in a large sketchy way, of the artistic milieu she wishes to produce, but a very hazy idea of how it is to be brought about.

There is, in the masculine mind, however, a deep-seated suspicion that an artistic home means an uncomfortable one. The very word " artistic " brings to his mind a picture of a room crowded with pictures and gimcracks, with chairs too good for one's feet, and not strong enough to sit upon; or else he is chilled by the vision of that other type of the artistic room in which everything has been reduced to its lowest terms and only that is permitted which is not only decorative in itself but that fills a definite role in the carefully studied picture. Not a jonquil must be touched, not a chair moved. Nothing is admitted except on business. A pipe left on the mantel would throw the whole room off its balance. These rooms are refined, delightful, and thoroughly enjoyable — in other people's houses.

Perhaps the best rule for obtaining the happy medium that will bring the words " artistic " and " home " together is the well known one of William Morris: " Have nothing in your house that you do not know to be useful or believe to be beautiful," — and, we might add, not too much of that! It may be taken as another rule that practical requirements either in the furniture or its arrangement must never be sacrificed for the sake of appearance.

" Art for art's sake," may do well enough in the studio but should not be tolerated as a rule for the home.

Good taste should be something more than a connoisseur's knowledge of works of art; it should include as well a just appreciation of the relation of these works of art to their surroundings and to each other. The room of careful selection, arrangement and restraint of which we have spoken, is an ideal one when it possesses the added feeling of comfort and usefulness. But the artistic should be so interwoven with the practical that the result will reflect the natural refinement which is the possession of the owner.

It is in this that the trained designer may be of use to the owner of general culture who desires to surround himself with an atmosphere of refinement but who has not had the special training necessary to produce it. There are a great many sensitive people of culture who become heartily sick of cheap meretricious decoration, but who, lacking the opportunity or nice discrimination to obtain for themselves simple refinement, give up the fight, throw over artistic effort of every sort, and allow themselves to revert to decorative savagery. Perhaps we would better say that they still keep their eclecticism, but that their desire for honest simplicity fixes their choice on a crude sort of furniture that was the style in the Stone Age.

We may imagine the perfectly harmonious living-room of the Cave Dweller, with its cavernous rough stone fireplace, where he might roast an ichthyosaurus whole, his chairs of great hewn logs, and his table ware of chipped flint. He himself, a dirty Hercules in a lion's skin, fondles a club. There is no jarring note in this picture. It is a perfectly consistent expression. Everything is in scale. But what would be our impression if the owner were a dyspeptic commuter with a pink tie and creased trousers? Great, clumsy furniture made of scantlings and upholstered with cow-hide is a style of work which seeks to curry favor by advertising itself as simple, when primitive would be a better word. It seeks to be nothing, and so escapes being bad. This negative virtue certainly makes it more desirable than a great deal that may be had for the same price. If our purse be slim perhaps we cannot do better, but it is nothing of which we may be proud. We may think of a chair of this sort that it is the best we can get for five dollars, but not the best chair we can get. No piece of furniture that can be made by an indifferent workman with a hatchet in half a day, can have much claim to be taken seriously.

It is no use. Time will not turn back in his flight, and while we are bound to sympathize with those who are in revolt against the tawdriness which is so common, the remedy does not lie in flying to the other extreme. It is rather in insisting on having our things well designed and well built, whether they be simple or elaborate. Nor is this impossible. Such things are to be had, and the ability exists to make them more common and only waits for the demand to call it forth. The difference between good and bad here is not to be measured in dollars, but solely in the skill of the designer.

In adopting a type of work we must imbue ourselves thoroughly with the scale and spirit of that style. We may choose the robust or the delicate; we may work in the spirit of the English Tudor or of the Colonial. The adjectives used to describe these two opposite types of work will vary with the sympathies of him who speaks. Where one will say the English work is clumsy and brutal, and the Georgian chaste and delicate, another, cast in a temperamentally different mold, will call English work virile and honest, and the other timid and anaemic. We know what each means, and that these descriptions will fit either style at its best and worst.

It does not make so much difference in which manner we elect to build. The important thing is not to mix them. When the dainty and the bold are joined we have an epicene effect impotent and vulgar. The result is an architectural eunuch.

Paneling, together with tapestry and painting, is the oldest

A fireplace that is too near a door loses much of its appeal to our desire for privacy and comfort

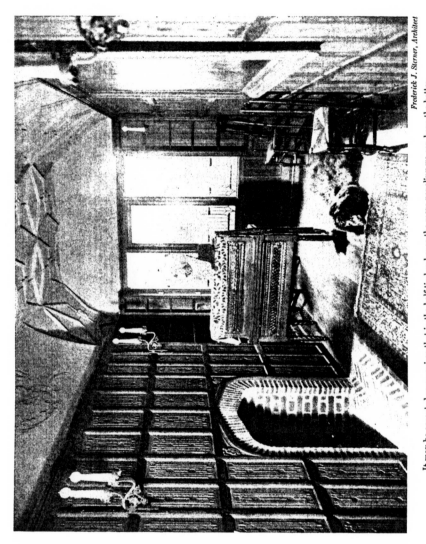

Frederick J. Sterner, Architect

It may be accepted as an axiom that in the half-timber house the more paneling we can have the better.
In this example the panels are carved with the linen-fold

method of covering the walls of a room. The chilliness and roughness of stone walls was what led to the use of hangings of some sort to keep out the drafts. Hides were *Wall* probably used first and later textiles of one sort *Treatment* or another. The weaving of tapestry for the especial purpose of wall covering was a very early and widespread industry throughout Europe and continued to supply a popular need well into the seventeenth century.

Paneling of one sort or another is also a very old art, and the various stages in its development are of great interest and worthy of study. Beginning with very wide panels of a single piece of wood, they were gradually made narrower as it became more difficult to get the larger pieces. Then the rails and stiles underwent a series of changes in their construction, all in the direction of economy of time and labor and the reducing of the necessary amount of skill required, so that a larger body of workmen would have access to the craft. This is of course the direction always taken in the improvement of methods of work.

It will not be worth our while here to discuss such technical improvements as molding " run " in the solid, or " planted " on. That is a matter of architectural archaeology. What we are interested in here is what our paneling is going to look like when we have it.

Few luxuries in a house will pay their cost better than wood paneling, but it has something to say for itself even on the score of economy. It is surprisingly warm, for it does not chill the warmed air of the room as plaster does, and we are saved the trouble and expense of constantly decorating, for unlike wall paper, paneling improves with age. The higher we can cover our walls with wood, the better they will look, and they will look best of all when sheathed in a brown coat from floor to ceiling.

While the divisions of the paneling should be of simple shape, ordinarily rectangular, we may well flower out at the top into something a little more interesting — a few simple moldings and perhaps a little carving; but if our room be not large we shall do well to keep the paneling very quiet and modest, avoiding too heavy sinkages or too heavy molding framing in the panels. If we use a lively wood, as quartered white oak or cypress, we need not fear monotony even if the panels have the slightest possible sinkage and no molding whatever. In fact, as in so many other problems in design, we are steering our course between the Scylla of fussiness on the one hand, and the Charybdis of stupidity on the other. The medium that is just in step with the room, its size, decoration and furnishing is what we are striving for.

For finish there is nothing so good as oil or wax on quartered oak over a brown stain, not too dark. Oak does not turn dark from age but only from dirt. In England the wood is frequently left as it comes from the plane, but in this country we prefer to do something by way of filling the pores in order to keep out the dampness. It is hardly necessary to discuss paper made to imitate wood and used to give the impression of paneling. It is among those lies that are the immoralities of architecture.

If we are to have plaster walls there is not much need to say anything about them here, as every man who lives in a house is familiar with them, or at least with the paper that usually covers them. It is not the author's intention to harangue against wall paper. Far from it. It is probably the most pleasant, attractive and serviceable covering for walls we have — for the money — and the variety of patterns should give us a new respect for the human mind. If the paper is one with flowers or trees it is safest to have them treated conventionally and to avoid the realistic roses, etc., which are pretty enough as pictures but are hardly suitable as a decoration. Papers printed in two tones of the same color are always safe and quiet and make excellent backgrounds for pictures.

It would be going a little too far afield to discuss the claims to our attention of the various sorts of patterns and colors. Choosing a paper is a matter in which we must keep one eye on the paper and the other on the room considered as a whole. The questions of color, of scale, and appropriateness of pattern, are the things to be considered, and with all the taste and knowledge in the world at our fingers' ends, it will still remain a most difficult thing to do, and most of us will have a surprise of some sort when we " see it on! "

There is much to be said for leaving plaster walls, and particularly ceilings, rough from the trowel or darby. They may then be tinted if thought desirable. The texture is soft and pleasing, and the reflected lights from the walls and ceilings much tempered. There is no better background for hanging pictures. It may seem rather ascetic to one who is used to having bunches of luscious pink roses nodding at him from his wall, but when he has become accustomed to it he will never go back to the other which he may well regard with a superior eye.

The simplest of all ceilings, which is the underside of the floor above, is still practicable for us if we choose. That is, the beams and joists forming the construction of *Ceilings* the floor are allowed to show from below, and the spaces between may be plastered or ceiled with wood. This gives us for beams the real solid timbers which are working for their living, and their checks and cracks and knots affect us pleasantly with the feeling which great strength in repose always gives. In the simplest work we may leave these untouched or enrich with carving or decorate in color as much as the room warrants. The objection (for no shield more inevitably has two sides than an architectural problem) is that such a floor is apt to transmit the noises from above, unless this contingency is guarded against. This may be prevented by laying sheathing quilt between the under and upper floors above, doing away as much as possible with any connection between the two, even to nailing from one into the other. The upper floor may be laid on sleepers and so floated on the quilt without even a nail to convey the vibrations to the under floor and its joists. Our plaster underneath may be also furred out onto the beams instead of being put on lathing nailed tight against the underflooring, thus giving us a dead-air space between the two which will help smother the sound waves.

If, however, this matter of sound seems to us a very important one and we are perhaps to have a young person above our heads who insists on taking a constitutional before going to bed, there is another way. This is to have our floor and ceiling constructed in the ordinary way, plaster and all, and then beam our ceiling without regard to what is behind. These false beams give us a greater freedom in the matter of design as we may be quite independent of any constructional requirements, as they are already taken care of. We may make our beams of any size or shape that suits us, space them and pattern the ceiling with them as we please. In this case, too, we may build them up instead of using the solid wood and so get rid of any future checks or cracks, if that is ever a desideratum. A still more thorough method of sound-proofing is to hang a false ceiling below the real one and entirely independent of it.

Now let us consider plaster ceilings of a more elaborate sort. The plaster ribbed ceilings of the time of Elizabeth and James are the most peculiarly and distinctively English things of all the architectural work of that busy time. Although the art was learned from the Italians, its subsequent development was along the lines of native thought and predilection. It clung to its individuality with great tenacity and refused to be touched by the foreign influence that was having such a marked effect all around it. The plasterers of this time developed a style of work that is peculiar to England and is found nowhere else. These ceilings are very elaborate and of most intricate pattern, being covered with an all-over design of interlaced and decorated bands and ribs, often with bosses or pendants at the intersections.

The effect of these complex ceilings when well designed and covering rooms worthy to receive them, is at once refined and sumptuous. When badly done they are extremely clamorous and chaotic.

The expense of doing this work to-day keeps it from being

more generally seen. There is, however, a simpler form of plaster decoration without its expense or its esthetic dangers, that might be much more commonly employed than it is. That is the application of molded ornament of a repeat pattern, used to accent structural lines such as the groins of vaults, or to serve as borders. Very pleasant and individual effects may be obtained in this way and it is to be hoped it will gain in favor. Facing page 103 is an example of this work.

There are two schools of technique in plaster work: the old cast work with its flat surfaces and blunt edges left untouched from the mold, and that other sort of work which is cut with a chisel as sharply and crisply as a cameo, with much undercutting — the whole full of life and snap. Some of the best work of this sort is to be seen at Fontainebleau and in many another palace throughout France and Italy, but not so often in England and never until the time of Inigo Jones. For our purposes in our modest homes we shall do better to use the molded decoration left untouched by the chisel, and not insist on the more nervous and habile style.

Vaulted ceilings are a pleasant variation and serve to bring a ceiling down in appearance. The curve may be either the arc of a circle or half an ellipse. If designed with groins, a pleasant feeling of solidity results, and an agreeable play of light and shade.

We have already seen how our first fireplace was a few flat stones with the opening in the roof protected from the weather

Fireplaces for the exit of the smoke. While this method may have given more heat to the room than the modern arrangement, it unquestionably must have given more smoke. The idea, first, of a great hood to catch it, and second, of a flue to guide it up and out, followed. The flue was naturally built against the wall and so the fire found itself there as well. Remembering that the logician has been described in derision as one who builds bridges across chasms over which any one can jump, we will hasten to assume that the reader can jump from the fire to the mantel, and not delay to follow the slow evolution of a shelf for pots and pans and on to such elaborate mantel arrangements as that shown facing page 111.

It is a long time since England has been a country where it was feasible to fill the great yawning fireplaces with logs of wood. As in all the old countries, wood is too precious to burn except in the most gingerly fashion, and with its disappearance the fireplace has shrunk until it is now too often only large enough to hold a small coal grate. So we shall not care for the modern English method of fireplace treatment, and would much better look to the old ones for inspiration.

As the function of a fireplace is bound to make it a focus of life in winter, so the treatment due to its importance will make it the decorative centre of the room the rest of the year. Whatever the details, its general design should be carefully kept on the same plane with the rest of the room and its furnishings. That is, it should be as simple or as gorgeous as its surroundings, whichever the case may be. The keynote that has been struck must be maintained if we are to have harmony. This might seem to be a superfluous warning to intelligent people, and would be so if widespread interest in the fireplace did not so often blind the owner to its less important surroundings. The owner has seen some particular fireplace somewhere which he admired so much that he has never forgotten it, and has long been awaiting the chance to reproduce it. So, with a single eye to its charms and no thought of the rest of his room, in it goes. There seems to be no other explanation why in a gentle, refined room we may turn around and find ourselves confronted by a ruffianly-looking cobble-stone fireplace, mantel and all. The sort of thing that would do very well in a bungalow with tables made of logs and armchairs ingeniously evolved from mutilated mackerel tubs, is not at all the thing to go with our Georgian furniture and white paint. Another abomination in a real house is the rough brick chimney and mantel, the tentacles of which seem to have insinuated themselves firmly about the hearts of our home-makers.

So, then, let us have our fireplace and mantel in step with us and our other belongings. The fireplace opening should be from two to five or six feet in width, with whatever height we choose. Three feet is enough width for an average room. The size of the flue must increase with the size of the opening; the sectional area should not be less than one-tenth of the area of the fireplace opening. A good depth for the opening is twenty inches. If it is deeper we lose too much of the heat, if shallower than sixteen inches we may have smoke. It is a mistake to have fireplaces over four feet wide unless we are prepared to burn big sticks, as small ones will look mean.

We may frame in the opening with either cut stone, as in the illustration facing page 106, or brick or tile, or anything that is not inflammable. If our mantel is of wood it must be kept at least four inches away all around. Red brick makes an excellent border in the living-room for unpretentious work. If brick is used in the bedrooms it will often be better to use some lighter color such as gray or yellow. When red brick is used the joints should always be either white or black, but the mortar should never be colored to match the bricks unless for some special reason. Tile gives a little more finished appearance than brick, but great care should be exercised in the selection. Excellent dull-glazed tile in plain colors are to be had. Those with the high gloss are generally to be avoided; the glitter of their high-lights gives a thin, hard look, which is a restless note in the room. Tiles without any glaze whatever may be had in quaint and attractive patterns, copies of medieval tile, and should be particularly suited to an English room. Stone, marble and cement facings are also used, the choice depending on the type of room with which we have to do.

The mantel is capable of such an inexhaustible variety of treatment that we can only speak of it in general terms. If the chimney breast is in the centre of the wall of a room not too high-studded, and is of ample width, it is never a mistake to insist on the horizontal lines of a mantel. In the first place the shelf may be carried straight across the front of the breast and even turn the corners, if our chimney projects into the room, and return on the sides against the wall. The space below the shelf on either side of the opening may be treated with some arrangement of panels, columns, brackets, or pilasters, and the space above, if we can afford an overmantel, either with simple paneling to the ceiling, or more elaborate work, if the general treatment of the room demands it. When finished, if we have managed to keep our horizontal feeling predominant, it will have a very sober, restful look. There is a sense of physical weight about such a design, a feeling of inertia, that is a very soothing one to tired nerves. A good picture framed into the overmantel looks well, much better than a mirror.

It is as true of the mantel as of the paneling, on whose province it begins to encroach, that the more the better. We cannot have too much wood, and if the question were asked if it would be better to have a great deal of cheaply done paneling or a little of very excellent quality, the author, after mature deliberation, decides that he would refuse to answer!

A common mistake with a fireplace that is to be much used as a centre of sociability, is to place lights over the mantel shelf. When these are lighted those in front of the fire will have to look directly at them, which is always disagreeable. If however such outlets are sufficiently supplemented by others, so that they may be treated merely as decorations if need be, and their light dispensed with, it may be a help in the design to keep them, and let their use be chiefly that of contributing to the general illumination on special occasions.

The stairs of an earlier age, which were of stone and wound around a central shaft or newel in a tower, are now rarely found.

Stairs Those between two walls are more common, but for front stairs are generally avoided. The stair that follows the walls, either straight or turning with the angles of the hall, were the latest invention and the best. They are capable of much dignity and richness in their treatment,

An old room in King's Head Inn where Dickens wrote "Barnaby Rudge." The English seem predisposed to the small basket-grate fireplace, perhaps on account of the scarcity of wood

The China Room, Holland House — a typical example of the Jacobean fireplace enriched to the extreme

The dining-room fireplace at Baddesley. Clinton, typical in its carving and the absence of a mantel-shelf

and lend an interest to the apartment in which they occur that transcends that of any other feature of the house. A stair is really only a luxurious ladder, having stringers instead of sides, and flat treads and risers instead of rungs. The hand-rail would have been called an effete and degenerate invention by the Lake Dwellers, and the balusters a waste of time and material which would have, no doubt, been bitterly assailed by the leaders of the Society for the Conservation of the Natural Resources of the time.

This ladder, as it becomes more elegant and complicated, should add to its other improvements that of diminishing in steepness. The amateur planner will nowhere have so much difficulty as with the stairs, and nothing short of bitter experience will teach him that they are one of the comparatively few things that will absolutely admit of no compromise. There is no standard width for halls or doors, no given size for fireplaces or rooms; they may be varied to suit. Not so our stairs. They are rigid and intractable. As long as men persist in growing six feet tall, they must have six feet of clear unobstructed space to walk in. While their legs are three feet long they will object to having to lift their bodies more than six or seven inches at a step. And if a man's foot is not quite twelve inches, it is so near it that nothing less than that much space will do for him to step on. There are various empirical rules for laying out comfortable stairs. One in common use with stair builders is that the product of the rise and tread must be between seventy-two and seventy-five inches, with the height of the tread between four and eight inches. Another rule in use in England gives the product as sixty-six inches, with the assumption that the rise will be five and a half inches, and this is further modified by the rule that for every one inch of tread added to or subtracted from twelve inches, the five and a half inch rise shall be diminished or increased by half an inch. That is, a rise of six inches should have a tread of eleven inches, a rise or seven inches, one of nine inches.

It will be seen from this rule that as the rise increases the tread decreases, and this is found to be a correct relation. It should be said in this connection that short flights of steps outdoors should have a wider tread, allowing for the longer stride which our greater pace will make necessary. This is also true where two or three steps occur alone inside. A very good proportion for comfort is a rise of five or six inches and a tread of fourteen or twelve.

The easy, luxurious stair, if one may ever call the exercise of lifting oneself by one's calves a luxury, of our old houses, is nowadays too often replaced by fewer and higher steps with the accompanying narrow tread. Whether this is due altogether to the rush of modern life which is willing to sacrifice anything to speed, and regards the elimination of one step as a gain in efficiency, or whether it is due partly to lack of floor space for the accommodation of a proper stair, is a question that might admit of debate. It is always appalling when our plan is still on paper, to see the amount of room the stairs take up, when they are properly drawn to scale. They are apt to so fill our hall and encroach on doors and passage space that we feel something must be done to keep them within bounds, forgetting that they are incompressible, and that the penalty of trying to squeeze them is sure to be hard climbing or knocking one's head, or more likely both. The steepness of some flights sometimes tempts one to think that the plush hand cord along the wall might well be used to rope the climbers together before they start up.

It is well not to go the whole distance from floor to floor without a landing where one may pause for a moment if desired. Old people find a long, uninterrupted flight a considerable tax on their strength, and such a chance to get their breath is much appreciated. If the stairs make a turn it should be by means of a landing, and never by the use of "winders" if it can be avoided. Winders are steps which have their risers radiating from a newel and are of necessity narrow at the newel, and flaring out against the opposite wall. This variation in width, together with the changing of direction, makes them the cause of many accidents.

The staircase is the one part of the house that we may not cramp with impunity. Here as elsewhere we cannot have too much paneling

Wilson Eyre, Architect

The living-room in a modern American home, where advantage has been taken of the decorative opportunities in a high ceiling and a gallery

There is, however, this to be said in their favor, that their varying width of tread, according to the distance from the newel, enables long or short legs to pick out the step that best suits them, and this one will unconsciously do in climbing a winding stair. We must expect to find winders in service stairs, where landings would be too high a price to pay for the space they require.

The English type of stairway that will be appropriate in our house will not vary in construction from any other, except in the one point of having what is called a " close string," that is, the outer edge of the stair, instead of allowing the risers and treads to be seen from below, is finished so that they are entirely enclosed, showing a straight edge parallel to the soffit. The balusters, which will be all of the same length, rest on this string. This is as typical of the English stair as the " open string," in which the ends of the steps show, is typical of the Georgian or Colonial work.

As for the rest, we shall have turned balusters, a heavy carved newel, and the finish generally will partake of the character and scale of the surrounding work, which will naturally be more heavy and robust than in the Colonial.

The chairs of the Tudor period were made entirely of wood, and though we may mitigate their rigidity somewhat with the help of cushions, we shall still find them heavy, clumsy *Furniture* and uncomfortable affairs, and unsuited to modern ideas. The tables with their bulbous legs do well enough, and many of the cabinets and presses of the period with their naïve carving are very quaint and charming. The cane furniture of the Stuarts and the turned work of the Jacobean period are thoroughly practical for us, and a sterling style of work that strikes the happy medium between the clumsiness of the early work and the almost rococo quality of what followed. In selecting our furniture we need not be too careful to insist on having everything of any one historic style. An anachronism will not be felt if we keep the same spirit and character in the work. Stuffed chairs, upholstered in leather or tapestry, the high repoussé, leather-backed Portuguese chairs, or even the armchairs of Italy, will not jar. Their fundamental characteristics are the same. Oscar Wilde has said: " All beautiful things belong to the same period," and if truth is somewhat stretched for the sake of the epigram, it is true so far as there is a bond of brotherhood, a secret understanding, between beautiful works of art, whatever their period or country. Of course with the " period room " there is no problem of this sort. But we need not feel because we have a couple of chairs of one period, that the whole room and its contents must be made to match.

It is more dangerous to mix our periods than to mix our nationalities. Work of the same epoch is apt to have much the same character everywhere. A Jacobean chair is perfectly compatible with one of Louis XIII in France, but will never do with a Louis XV chair, or even with an English chair of the time of George III.

There is one article of furniture, however, over the style of which we have no control, namely that amorphous monstrosity, the grand piano. Its portentousness begins with its name and is further evidenced by the great, shapeless body supported on its fat, vulgar legs, its unspeakable " piano finish " still further calling attention to its grandeur. On entering a strange room if we are in an absent-minded mood, our first instinctive thought on noticing its funereal presence will be that we must not intrude at a time like this when the family's late pet mastodon is evidently lying in state. It is one of the seven wonders of the decorative world why it is that civilization has put up with such a thoroughly outrageous piece of furniture for so long. Perhaps it is because one unconsciously thinks of the ugly woman with the beautiful voice, and with a sigh classes it as another one of the mysterious workings of nature. But it is not a necessity at all. Splendid piano cases have been designed, but it is only spasmodically that the heavy hand of the Victorian era has been for a moment shaken off. To have a case especially designed means that we shall have no choice in selecting the tone of the piano but must take

" the works " as it comes; and there is of course a great choice in the tone of pianos even of the best makers.

There is no more delightful study in the decorative arts than that of furniture. Men of all ages have gloried in lavishing their best energies and skill on the artistic invention and beautifying of the articles in daily use. Men have always expressed their true selves in the work they loved best to do. Of old furniture it is not too much to say: Show me what a man sits on and I will tell you what he is.

The subject of the styles of furniture is not one to be treated lightly or dismissed in a paragraph, and is far beyond the scope of any such general work as this.

Public education in matters of architecture and decorative taste have made gigantic strides in the last twenty years. In nothing do we show the characteristics of a quick-thinking, adaptable people as in the eager reception we give this renaissance of the arts in which we have had so large a share. No better architecture is being done anywhere in the world to-day than in this country, and if some of the allied arts lag a little behind we feel that it will not be for long; for ability and enthusiasm are at work, and the result will be beauty in the service of man.

THE UNIVERSITY PRESS, CAMBRIDGE, U. S. A.